"We want to be more involved in our services ... to have a more powerful say in our lives ... For people with learning difficulties to be more independent in themselves, like ordinary citizens, to have their own rights."

(Richard Maylin of Hertfordshire People First and POhWER, in a letter to the author)

"We don't see any of the bigwigs ..."

"I think a visit from the bosses would be good, to see their faces."

(tenants in supported housing)

"... they should listen to us more ..."

(person with learning difficulties at a user forum)

Acknowledgements

As is often the case with such exercises, if the contribution of all those involved was given due recognition, the acknowledgements would be almost as long as the text itself. I can only offer my profound thanks to all the individuals (some who are mentioned in the text, and some who are not) who assisted me. I would not have been able to do my job were it not for the fact that so many people continue to be so unstintingly helpful.

I would also like to thank the many organisations and agencies who were so willing to put ideas about participation into practice. These include:

British Institute of Learning Disabilities
Change
Gloucestershire Health Authority and the Shadow Group
Greater Glasgow Health Board
Hackney Social Services
Hertfordshire Social Services and POhWER
Knowsley Metropolitan Borough Council
Leeds Coalition
National Development Team
Oxfordshire Social Services
People First, Cardiff and the Vale
Phoenix NHS Trust
Staffordshire Social Services
Swindon People First
West Surrey Health Authority

However, some contributions should be acknowledged directly. I am extremely grateful to John Harris of the British Institute for Learning Disabilities, both for commissioning the work in the first place and for being so tolerant of its (very) slow gestation. As ever, Linda Holley has done sterling work interpreting my attempts to write. My proof reader and editor likes to remain anonymous, but I would particularly like to thank her for undertaking the rather thankless task of cutting down the original unwieldy manuscript by nearly half. Finally, I would like to record my appreciation of my colleagues at the Norah Fry Research Centre, for helping to create and maintain such a pleasant working environment.

Ken Simons
August 1998

The preparation of this report was funded by a Department of Health grant to BILD.

Contents

Chapter 1: Setting the Scene

Background

This book draws on a number of different sources of information, ideas and experience. These include:

- Interviews and discussions with a range of individuals and organisations.

This book is very much a collaborative effort. Its existence is testimony to a willingness on the part of a wide range of individuals and organisations to share their experiences. Some responded to an advert in the BILD newsletter *Advantage* seeking examples of participation, others were identified through informal networking. While some had established a reputation for working with users, others were taking their first tentative steps in this direction. However, all were prepared to give unstintingly of their time. A list of organisations and agencies involved is included in the acknowledgements.

- The literature on participation.

There is now a considerable body of material that deals with different aspects of participation, or participation in specific contexts. Some of this material relates directly to services for people with learning difficulties. However, an effort has also been made to include examples from other contexts. This is partly because some important initiatives (for example, the development of direct payments and personal assistant schemes) have, hitherto, rather passed learning disability services by. Equally, however, many services are managed 'generically', and there is increasing interest in services that are not 'impairment specific'. To keep the book as readable as possible, direct references in the text have been minimised. However, for those who are interested, the Bibliography includes an additional list of 'other material'.

- The direct experience of the author.

The author has been directly involved in a number of studies that have focused on participation issues, including research on the experience of people involved in self and citizen advocacy, complaints procedures, and more recently, tenant participation in supported housing. Further, in a personal capacity, the author has both acted as an advisor to a People First group, been a member of a circle of support, and acted as a crisis advocate.

Aims

The aim of this book is to promote the development of participation within the commissioning and purchasing of services for people with learning difficulties, through:

● identifying the principles underlying participation;

● setting these principles in the context of the commissioning and purchasing process;

● providing some examples of participation in practice;

● promoting links between people involved in participation;

● exploring possible directions in participation.

While targeted at people involved in commissioning and purchasing, this book should also be of interest to service providers. In many instances, people with learning difficulties will need the active assistance of front-line staff to access events set up by commissioners or purchasers. Conversely, any effective participation strategy set up by providers will inevitably also involve helping people with learning difficulties to have a voice in the wider structures, including those concerned with commissioning and purchasing.

Why participation?

Although many people now accept the case for participation, it is worthwhile beginning by rehearsing the arguments in its favour. These take three basic forms:

1. participation is a moral imperative
To be involved in making decisions about one's life is a fundamental part of being a citizen, and the role of services is to help enable people to play their part as citizens. As a moral imperative, there is, therefore, a case for participation regardless of its effects; people should be involved in decision making even if it makes life more complicated.

2. participation makes for better services
Most people involved would also argue that effective participation makes for better services. Services which are geared to the wishes of those who use them are likely to be more aware of, and focused on, the reality of people's lives. They will be more responsive, flexible and efficient, providing help when people want it and need it, and not when they do not.

There are all kinds of positive spin-offs to be gained from a more equal relationship, but perhaps the greatest significance of this shift is the element of protection it affords. Neglect and abuse by service providers is still far too common in services for people with learning difficulties. We still do not know that much about the factors that put people at risk. However, as Ann Craft (Craft, 1996) has suggested, these are likely to include services where there is a culture of compliance, and greater dependence on staff by people who use services.

The less the relationships between users and professionals are characterised by dependency and compliance on the part of the former, the better protected people will be. That *must* mean taking participation seriously.

Hilary Brown has worked extensively on the issues of the sexual abuse of people with learning difficulties and she notes (Brown, 1996) that people with learning difficulties are at increased risk of sexual and other crimes against the person:

> *"There is a balance to be struck about how to acknowledge and take into account the vulnerability of people with learning disabilities while upholding their right to make choices. The debate is often framed in terms of empowerment versus protection, but actually people need both."*

3. participation can have a positive impact on people with learning difficulties
By encouraging people with learning difficulties to become more confident and assertive, to take more responsibility for themselves and others, to make choices and to have more control over their lives, to be less dependent on others, and to be more informed, an effective participation strategy has the potential to make a significant impact on the way people with learning difficulties see themselves.

Given that many services have similar aims, one might have expected them to see participation as a high priority. However, Monica Keeble (1996) found that tenant participation in supported housing was often seen as a 'luxury' only to be considered once the basics were in place:

> *"Something we will prioritise when our staff are not so busy."*

This is a widespread, but ultimately short-sighted view. If the aim of a service is to encourage independence and promote self-esteem, then participation issues need to be at its core.

The significance of participation within a commissioning and purchasing strategy

Most of the existing material on participation is directed at service providers. This is not unreasonable; front line services should be responsive to the wishes and needs of those who use them. However, it is no longer enough for participation to be seen as solely the preserve of the providers, since their room for manoeuvre is often limited by the demands of the purchasers.

The crucial players in deciding what services should be provided are the commissioners and purchasers, but so far there have been few attempts to involve people with learning difficulties in this decision making beyond limited 'consultation' about published 'community care' plans.

Yet there are very good reasons why commissioners and purchasers should adopt a comprehensive participation strategy:

1. commissioners and purchasers are often 'remote' from the day-to-day reality of services
Decisions are made without an awareness of how users experience services. This can particularly be the case in the NHS, where, at the point of split between purchasers and provider functions, many of the people with direct experience of services end up in provider units. As a result, many commissioners and purchasers have to rely heavily on providers for information.

2. commissioners and purchasers cannot separate needs from wishes
The key role of commissioners is to identify the needs of the population they serve and ensure that there are services to meet those needs. However, in practice it is impossible to envisage how this would be done without taking into account the views of people with learning difficulties, both in terms of what their needs are (what actually matters to them) and how services respond to them. This is particularly so when dealing with 'social care'.

3. commissioners and purchasers face an imbalance of accountability
Commissioners and purchasers serve many kinds of groups and are held to account in many different ways. There should be structures to ensure that the views of providers, Councillors, NHS Trust Directors and families are all heard, but the paradox is that the very people for whom the services seek to provide often have little or no voice in these structures. This leads to an imbalance of accountability.

4. commissioners and purchasers should have a role in ensuring that providers take participation seriously
This can be done directly, both through the contracting process and through regulation, and indirectly, by establishing a wider framework involving user participation as an integral element.

5. commissioners and purchasers are expected to involve users and carers
In case any commissioners and purchasers are not convinced by the above arguments, it is worth adding that user and carer participation is not an optional extra. There is extensive official guidance (for example SSI, 1991a) which seeks to ensure that the voices of users and carers are heard by people responsible for developing services.

What do we mean by purchasing or commissioning?

A detailed discussion of commissioning and purchasing could fill the entire report, so only a brief outline is included here. Those wishing to pursue the issue further might care to read the BILD Seminar papers on the subject (see Harris, 1996).

The commissioning cycle

'Commissioning' is the term given to the overall process of linking the strategic functions of statutory authorities (for example, community care planning), with the tactical process of putting strategic plans into operation. In contrast, 'purchasing' is very specifically concerned with the process of linking users to services, through tasks like selecting providers, contracting, and care management. The phrase 'commissioning and purchasing' is therefore used here to convey both the general (strategic) and the specific.

Commissioning is often described in terms of a cyclical process (see Greig, 1997). Within this it is possible to identify three distinct phases:

1. developing a strategic framework for services
This first phase of the cycle is concerned with developing and articulating a clear vision of how services should work. This needs to be set out in terms of the kinds of needs that are to be met, and the overall resources available to be deployed. There will be critical decisions to be made that will have a direct bearing on the lives of people with learning difficulties. For example, what are the weaknesses in local services, and what will be the priorities for future development or reforms? The decisions made at this phase in the cycle will either close off or open up opportunities. The development of strategic vision, therefore, is an obvious place to start when involving people with learning difficulties in purchasing and commissioning (see Chapter 3).

2. operational planning and purchasing
Less rarefied but equally important, this second phase of the commissioning cycle is concerned with implementing strategic plans. Again, there will be critical decisions made which will directly affect the people who use services. Many of these decisions will concern straightforward, concrete issues that are relatively easy for people with learning difficulties to understand and to get involved in (see Chapter 4).

3. reviewing and monitoring services

The reviewing and monitoring of services is a much neglected area. Yet if the lessons from existing service provision are to be learnt, and then fed back into the next turn of the commissioning cycle, this final phase should be just as important as those preceding it. Judgements about what constitutes good or bad services are difficult to make without relation to the experiences and views of those using them. Similarly, with limited resources it will be nigh on impossible to monitor what is happening on a day-to-day basis in services, without engaging with users (and their supporters) as partners in the exercise. One of the best ways of protecting vulnerable people is to ensure they know their rights and what to expect from services, and how to speak up about any concerns they have (see Chapter 5).

The structure of this report reflects these three distinct phases, with a chapter devoted to each in turn. For each, the aim is to highlight the opportunities for participation which exist in each phase.

Joint commissioning

It is now increasingly rare to find an area which does not have some kind of joint commissioning arrangement for learning disability services, bringing together the NHS and the local authority. However, Rob Greig, Co-director of the Community Care Development Unit at King's College in London, argues that while there may be much better communication between health and local authority purchasers than in the past, there are still doubts about how often this translates into a genuine joint purchasing strategy.

Of course, as Greig points out, joint commissioning is not an end in itself. Rather, it represents an attempt to overcome the inconsistent and arbitrary divides which continue to plague services. The driving vision behind joint commissioning is of a network of services which:

- offer a full range of support options reflecting the needs of the individuals, not organisational boundaries;

- are based on common values with common assessment processes;

- deploy all the available resources in an efficient and transparent manner, ensuring that they are effectively targeted;

- are effectively monitored, with information about outcomes fed back into the planning process.

However, while joint commissioning offers considerable scope for participation, in practice this is an area where little progress has been made. Greig comments:

> "*Attempts to involve users and carers have met with limited success. The more interesting examples are possibly where user and carer structures are managed and controlled by those users and carers, and are a mechanism to inform the commissioners of people's needs and wishes, rather than a tokenistic representation on a commissioning group.*"

(Greig, 1997)

The way joint commissioning (indeed commissioning and purchasing in general) is organised is likely to make participation either easier or harder, depending on the circumstances. Two issues stand out in particular:

1. pro-active or laissez-faire

> "*If all we do is water the garden we may end up with, not a garden, but a weed patch. In the same way purchasers cannot merely wave money and service specifications around. Talent must be seeded and nurtured ...*"

(Duffy, 1996)

Market-led, laissez-faire approaches to purchasing will offer rather fewer opportunities for participation, compared with a more pro-active approach, with commissioners and purchasers promoting an active dialogue between purchasers, providers, and actual or potential users.

2. the importance of a shared vision

> "*If there is no shared common purpose between organisations, there is little chance of joint commissioning achieving the desired goals - in fact it may exacerbate difficulties.*"

(Greig, 1997)

In many instances, a common vision does not exist within agencies, let alone between them. This means that joint commissioning structures are often a forum for resolving long-standing and entrenched conflicts and this is not an ideal environment for trying to involve people with learning difficulties or their families.

However, there are circumstances in which the imperative of working out ways to involve people with learning difficulties might help concentrate minds, leading to genuine joint commissioning. Similarly, a shared understanding of the realities of the lives of people with learning difficulties, and their hopes and aspirations, might well assist in developing a shared vision for services. As one purchaser commented:

> *"We are using a focus on individuals [with a learning difficulty] to restore rationality."*

Terminology

It is increasingly fashionable to adopt the term 'empowerment' rather than 'participation' or 'involvement'. This can be more than just a semantic nicety; often the shift in terminology has been accompanied by an attempt to move beyond the relatively limited 'participation' options previously on offer, towards a more radical vision of an entirely new relationship between people who use services and the professionals who work in them: a relationship based on partnership, rather than dependency and compliance. On the whole that vision is to be embraced.

However, the shift in terminology is perhaps less welcome, not because empowerment is an undesirable outcome (quite the contrary), but precisely because it is an outcome. If people are empowered by a process, fine; but *they* need to be the judges of whether or not that is the case. Many of the things that have previously gone under the heading of 'involvement' turned out to be a distinctly disempowering experience for those directly involved (Lindow and Morris, 1995).

Empowerment implies both having more control over events and, as a consequence, experiencing feelings of increased self-esteem and confidence. Yet to be involved in a process which appears to make little difference in services, which is boring or alienating in some way, risks having the opposite effect. To label a process as 'empowerment' is to make assumptions about the outcome of that process. The danger of such labels is that they also have a sort of self-promoting quality. We need to be critical about the *effects* of what we do; the advantage of using terms like 'involvement' or 'participation' is that they stick to describing the process, they do not carry implicit predictions about their effects.

Chapter 2: The Idea of 'Participation'

This chapter explores the principles of participation. It asks what changes are needed to ensure that people with learning difficulties have a voice, both individually and collectively. It draws on an extensive literature on participation and advocacy, pointing out the general lessons to be learnt from past experience.

The key principle of participation is neatly summed up in a phrase used by the organisation Advocacy in Action:

> *Nothing about me without me.*

This does not mean that people with learning difficulties *have* to attend every meeting, nor indeed are most people with learning difficulties likely to be interested in every aspect of organising services. Professionals should, however, be accountable to people with learning difficulties for all the significant decisions that get made in relation to services. Therefore, *all* aspects of commissioning and purchasing services should be considered as potential opportunities for participation.

Does participation really make a difference to people's lives? We would argue very clearly, yes. However, even as advocates of participation, we have to acknowledge that there have been examples where considerable resources and time and energy have been put into developing complex participation structures which had little *apparent* effect.

It can take a long time to change services, and the effects of participation might not be apparent in the short to medium term. These are not arguments for not trying things. There are, however, good reasons to look critically at participation initiatives and ask some searching questions:

- Does the initiative focus on the issues that matter to people with learning difficulties?

- Does the initiative have the potential to help change services for the better?

- How will we need to respond to the initiative?

- Is there support for it to be effective?

Complex questions and dilemmas

Anyone involved in developing or implementing participation strategies will soon discover all kinds of questions and dilemmas being posed, often with no obvious right answers. Rather, there will be different considerations that need to be balanced against each other. This section raises some of these questions and explores their wider implications.

The implication of diversity

A recognition of the *diversity* of people with learning difficulties is fundamental. People with a learning difficulty:

- come from very different cultures and backgrounds;
- have had very different past experiences;
- have very different strengths and capacities;
- have quite different values and beliefs.

What will suit some will not necessarily suit others. For example, many people with learning difficulties draw great strength from being part of the self-advocacy movement, yet others are extremely uncomfortable in a group, and opt out of collective activities. For participation to be inclusive, we need to learn from all people with learning difficulties and find ways of both recognising and *celebrating* their diversity. There would need, therefore, to be diverse ways of participating.

People's disagreements about what they want from services (as though professionals never disagreed!) are unfortunately sometimes taken as an argument *against* involving them. Yet there will inevitably be conflicts of interest between groups of users (and non-users, see box below), and the system needs to recognise this.

Equal opportunities issues

Most 'user involvement' initiatives focus on people who are already users of the service. Yet we know that some minority ethnic groups are systematically under-represented in services (Emerson and Hatton, 1998). There is a risk that in failing to draw into the participation process people who do not use services (because the latter do not meet their needs), the cultural insensitivity of services will be reinforced. Similarly, the traditional networks of voluntary organisations and users' groups who are consulted on services may well not include newer organisations or groups based in minority ethnic communities. The solution, according to Bewley and Glendinning (1994) is to adopt a 'community development approach'. This lack of involvement of people from particular ethnic groups was certainly a concern in Hackney. Members of the Orthodox Jewish and Muslim communities had all expressed concerns about

---

the lack of appropriate services. There are known to be relatively large Turkish and Kurdish communities in the borough, but relatively few users from these communities have been identified. The message coming from many of these communities stressed the importance of working with or through groups who had experience as members of those communities. As a result, Hackney worked with a number of independent sector organisations like Yad Voezer and Anika Patrice. Also, one plank of the local user involvement strategy involved ensuring that all community liaison officers were aware of the local citizen advocacy service.

Summary point: If participation strategies are to be inclusive they must target excluded groups; some kind of community development approach will be needed.

Sphere of influence: the importance of being outward looking

"Since services constitute only a small part of the life experience of most users, empowerment is far from being the sole preserve of services."

(Grant, 1997)

There is a tendency for professionals to divide the world up in ways that reflect the organisations in which they work. The way that participation is thought about and organised, therefore, inevitably reflects these divisions. In the field of learning disability this has created a primary focus on the immediate purchasers and providers of specialist services. However, if the issues are considered from the perspective of people who use these same services, they begin to look rather different.

To start with, for people with learning difficulties, organisational boundaries seem less important. Indeed, many people with learning difficulties will probably not be at all clear which organisations are responsible for which bits of the service. Also, while it is likely that service providers *will* loom large, there will be many other organisations which may be more significant. Secondly, services often do not reflect what is important in people's *lives*. Thirdly, the concerns of *services* will often barely touch on the wider social processes which leave people vulnerable or excluded in the first place.

To take the specific example illustrated in Figure 1, of a tenant living in supported housing, a whole range of organisations *could* be making decisions which either close down or open up opportunities. Note that while individuals or organisations on the outer ring of Figure 1 may have less significance on a day-to-day basis, they may well be making decisions that have profound effects on the lives of people with learning difficulties. By implication, participation is *not* just about involving people with learning difficulties in the immediate provision of specialist services, but also enabling them to have a wider voice and to influence organisations which can affect their *lives*. Therefore, any participation strategy needs to be outward looking, with efforts made to ensure that policy makers in the wider framework are made aware of the impact of their decisions on people with learning difficulties.

A European view

As EU directives begin to influence services in the UK, they have a direct impact on the lives of people with learning difficulties. *Europe People First* is a project in which self-advocates from groups all around the UK have got together with the aim of making links with self-advocacy groups from other countries, to find out what interests them and to exchange information. The hope is to form a council for Europe, which would be run and organised by self-advocates themselves, with the eventual aim of having some kind of voice, as citizens of Europe, within European affairs.

Currently, self-advocacy means many different things within the different cultures and countries of the European Union. Europe People First are actively looking for ways to meet their counterparts in other countries, to exchange ideas, and to promote human rights in Europe. Contact details for Europe People First are included in the resource section.

Figure 1: Spheres of influence

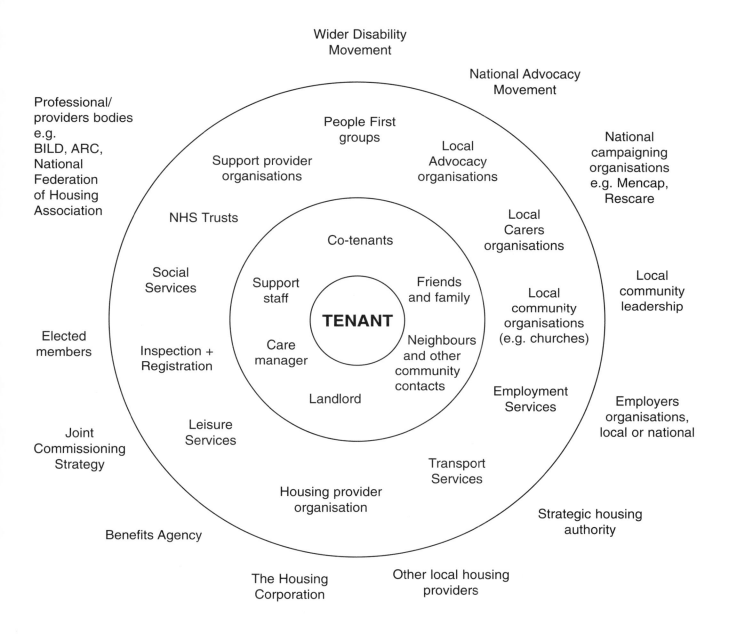

CENTRAL GOVERNMENT

EUROPEAN UNION

Wider Disability Movement

National Advocacy Movement

Professional/ providers bodies e.g. BILD, ARC, National Federation of Housing Association

People First groups

Local Advocacy organisations

National campaigning organisations e.g. Mencap, Rescare

Support provider organisations

NHS Trusts

Local Carers organisations

Social Services

Co-tenants

Support staff

Friends and family

Local community organisations (e.g. churches)

Local community leadership

Elected members

Inspection + Registration

Care manager

TENANT

Neighbours and other community contacts

Landlord

Joint Commissioning Strategy

Leisure Services

Employment Services

Employers organisations, local or national

Transport Services

Benefits Agency

Housing provider organisation

Strategic housing authority

The Housing Corporation

Other local housing providers

The implication of change

A commitment to participation means being prepared to change. Like everyone else, people with learning difficulties will sometimes be worried about change; they may prefer the 'known' rather than face uncertainty about what some alternative might mean. This has been an issue in day services. One authority approached current users while exploring some of the alternatives in a review of day services. Not surprisingly, this revealed interest in a number of options, including paid work. However, discussion of these alternatives quickly revealed that most resources were tied up in day centres, and that the development of alternatives on any scale could imply centre closures. This alarmed the users of the service, who started talking about a 'save our centre campaign' and began insisting that they did not want any changes.

While it is important to be honest about the risks associated with change, confusing the issue of what services people really wanted with the issue of how they might be achieved in the longer term was, in retrospect, an unwise strategy. The closure of centres might not have been the only option, and without a clear idea of what the alternatives might be, and what costs might be involved, it could be argued that such an assumption was premature. Introducing the issue of potential centre closure so early in the process made everyone defensive.

There are some important lessons to be learnt here. First, people with learning difficulties are likely to be worried about change if they lack clear vision of what is involved, and if their fears are not addressed. Secondly, participation will have important implications for the management of strategic change, and vice versa.

The issue of power

> "... consultation as empowerment is not about the transfer of
> power from professionals or administrators to users or families
> as if it were some zero sum game. Neither has it anything to do
> with historical bases of authority such as formal position, status,
> charisma or tradition. Rather it concerns the sharing of life
> experience, knowledge, information and insight between all
> members of the group as a whole ..."

(Grant, 1997)

If power is bestowed by factors such as income, education, life experience, status, access to support etc., then there is little question that service users have less 'power' than professionals. Any participation strategy has to address at least some of these differences in power at both individual and structural levels, so that people with learning difficulties are provided with some leverage over the way decisions are made.

There is an assumption that if people who use services become more powerful, then professionals will have to relinquish power to them. There is *some* truth in this proposition. For example, people who work in services where they get held to account are not free to behave like complete tyrants; their room for manoeuvre will have been limited, and, in this sense, they are less powerful. However, there are reasons to see such assumptions as too simplistic.

First, powerful looking structures (like Joint Planning Groups) often have less influence on events than might be expected. Even 'powerful' (high status) individuals often find it difficult to influence directly what happens in the front line. Conversely, everyone has *some* power; even the people who we might see as the least powerful - the service users - *can* be remarkably effective at 'resistance'.

Secondly, more power for some does not necessarily mean less power for others. There can be win-win situations as well as win-lose. For example, professionals working in an effective *alliance* with people with learning difficulties and their families *could* have more influence than if they simply worked on their own.

Thirdly, there is a risk of undervaluing some forms of participation. Some, usually those with a strong symbolic element (for example, having a seat on a management committee or a strategic planning group), are often seen as having higher status, while less obviously exciting examples get undervalued. This works to marginalise those who have difficulty participating in formal settings.

Representation

Inherent in the idea of participation is a commitment to a democratic approach to services. However, most of our experience of 'democracy' is bound up with representational systems which are essentially formal and which offer little direct involvement to the citizen. This creates a number of expectations about representation.

Bewley and Glendinning (1994) report that when local authority officers wanted to recruit 'user representatives' for planning teams they simply invited individuals known to them personally. Organisations of disabled people questioned how such individuals could fulfil a representative function without clear systems of selection and accountability.

There are a number of conflicting considerations here:

Users find themselves in a Catch-22 situation
If people with learning difficulties are articulate, their views are seen as 'unrepresentative' and are discounted. If they are not articulate, then their views either get discounted anyway, or others step in to speak for them.

Representation gets confused with representativeness
There is a case for sometimes looking for the 'typical' user. However, being representative (if that is ever really possible) is not the same as being a representative. People who are good at representing others are often atypical people, but we must not assume that someone more skilled and articulate is necessarily out of touch with their less articulate peers.

Service users who act as representatives are often judged by double standards
It is not unknown for personality clashes or power struggles within user-led organisations to alienate professionals, and to lead them to interpret such phenomena as indications of the incapacity of users to behave appropriately. However, few would try to pretend that such events never happen in professional organisations!

Professionals tend to define 'constituency' in service oriented terms
Perhaps not surprisingly, professionals have a service oriented view of the world. When they want to find 'user representatives', they naturally think in terms of people who use the service (the constituency) electing representatives to engage with. However, this risks marginalising independent user-led groups based outside services.

By contrast:

Representing others is a demanding job, which requires considerable skill
Developing an understanding of the issues for one's peers, representing those interests in formal contexts, feeding back information to one's peers, gauging their reaction and representing them further, is no easy job. Many people who get elected as representatives in all walks of life are not very good at it, and will find it easier (and are more effective) when reflecting their own experience.

Sometimes user-led organisations do argue against the interests of some users
The responsibility for judging the competing demands from people with learning difficulties remains with the professionals who manage services. Sometimes it is appropriate to question what user-led organisations say, but if professionals are going to challenge them, it should be on the basis of evidence; professionals should not assume they know what users of services think.

Where users are diverse, the task of representing them will be that much harder
Representing differing interests is difficult, and may highlight tensions between people who use services. The greater the conflict, the harder the task.

Ways of strengthening representation

A sensible strategy will need to recognise that formal representational structures will work best if actively supported. This could be achieved in a number of different ways:

Enabling people to be effective representatives
People can be encouraged to be effective representatives (formal or otherwise) and supported in a number of ways, including the provision of personal support and ensuring that training in the appropriate leadership skills is available.

Encouraging the development of organised constituencies
The more organised a constituency is, the easier it is to represent it, and the more likely that representatives will be held to account. It is important to help people with learning difficulties to organise themselves, for example by ensuring that user-led groups have access to joint funding.

Including marginalised groups
Mainstream views will emerge fairly easily; it is the concerns of minorities which are more likely to be excluded. Those responsible for taking a strategic view therefore have to take steps to ensure that minority opinion is heard.

People with learning difficulties or disabled people?

Should participation structures be developed specifically for people with learning difficulties, or should they be seen as part of the wider constituency of disabled people?

There are grounds for arguing that people with learning difficulties have at times lost out because they have not been included in the wider disability movement. The marginalisation of people with learning difficulties in personal assistant schemes would be a case in point (Simons and Ward, 1997). Equally, people with learning difficulties who get involved in wider forums often complain that their voice gets drowned out by those who are more articulate.

While people with learning difficulties will have many experiences in common with other disabled people, they are also likely to experience unique discrimination related to their intellectual capacity. They therefore need *both* to be part of a wider disability movement *and* to have space to develop their own voice.

Complexity

The commissioning and purchasing of services often includes activities which are inherently complex and there will be issues that many people with learning difficulties will have difficulty understanding. But that is not an argument for excluding them from the process. Even if people with learning difficulties may not comprehend the technical details, they are much more likely to be able to understand the implications of decisions, particularly as they impact on their lives. Similarly, discussing issues in the abstract makes them harder to relate to, while focusing issues around the concrete reality of people's lives makes it easier for them to make an effective contribution. The key, therefore, is dealing with the technical elements of the process in a way that does not overload people with learning difficulties, but leaves them with a broader understanding of what is happening. This clarification of processes and procedures, along with the provision of more accessible information, would be helpful to everyone.

Responsibilities as well as rights?

By definition, rights bring responsibilities. However, this can become complicated. While people with learning difficulties are subject to the same expectations and sanctions as everyone else, they will sometimes do things that make professionals uncomfortable. People who work with users will have to deal with a whole range of situations on a day-to-day basis, such as:

- Many groups will be quite intolerant of people with learning difficulties with challenging behaviour (often for understandable reasons) and this may lead them to act in ways which are exclusive rather than inclusive. At what point does this become unacceptable?

- Many people with learning difficulties will come from communities where racism and sexism are the norm. Sexist or racist behaviours will need to be challenged, but how far should we go in imposing values on people with learning difficulties that may be quite alien to them?

- Some people have difficulty learning certain social skills. This can be an issue, particularly where they may be meeting those who may have little direct contact with people with learning difficulties (like councillors or senior managers). Should 'rude' behaviour debar people from such meetings?

There are no simple answers to any of these questions. Most people manage by trying to work out what is most appropriate from the following set of basic principles.

- Apply consistent expectations to all participants at a meeting - 'ground rules'. For example, we often expect 'user representatives' to behave in almost idealised ways. Non-disabled people in the same context are often not challenged to the same extent.

- Be clear about expectations, and be prepared to negotiate within reasonable bounds.

- Support people to discharge their responsibilities.

- Be prepared to be challenged yourself; model good practice by being prepared to account for your own actions.

- Set holistic expectations which do not underestimate people's skills or put people under pressures that they cannot cope with.

- Work out how you can implement these suggestions beforehand. By helping people make connections between different kinds of behaviour, it may well be possible to develop some shared rules. Similarly, try to help people work out what the consequences of their actions will be.

Being committed to empowering people with learning difficulties does not mean that they should never be challenged; though any challenges need to be respectful and justified.

The practical implications of a coordinated participation strategy

While some of the dilemmas posed by developing participation are quite complex, many more straightforward practical lessons have also emerged from the participation literature.

The importance of independent advocacy

Independent advocacy allows people with learning difficulties to look outside the immediate services they use, for advice, information, support, encouragement, and in some cases, protection.

While we would not want to suggest that self-advocacy groups based within services have no value, they also have inevitable limitations, as it is difficult for them to look beyond the immediate environment of the service (see Dowson, 1997). There are many areas where independent advocacy is missing or ineffective and, in this context, any advocacy is better than none. Purchasers and providers need to take responsibility for ensuring that people have the best support available, even if this means compromises in the short-term.

The need for resources to be put into participation

A budget to support participation (for example for transport costs, personal assistance etc.) is essential: involvement in participation activities can be costly for both the individuals or groups targeted. Bewley and Glendinning (1994) found few examples of users being compensated for the costs incurred when taking part in planning meetings. They also found many organisations of disabled people beginning to question whether their involvement in community planning was worthwhile. Given the apparently limited impact of their contributions on final plans, the time and energy invested often seemed disproportionate.

Reimbursing people is not just about covering expenses; there will come a point where it is appropriate to pay people for their work, whether as individuals or by commissioning work from a group. Payment will raise all kinds of issues. At what point should people no longer be expected to do things on a voluntary basis? How much should people be paid, and how will it affect people who are on benefits? Given that payment changes the relationship between payer and payee, what impact will this have on the expectations of the person or persons with learning difficulty (and will some form of contract be needed)?

These difficult questions can be resolved if tackled early. Some consultation with local People First or self-advocacy groups, particularly if they have experience of employing members, would be a good starting point. As many groups become organised, they will also need access to office space or similar resources (for example, photocopying) along with support to use them.

It can't be business as usual

Most self-advocacy groups have stories about the time that one of their members was invited on to a committee or a planning group, and was then left to flounder. The problems are legion: no introductions or explanations for newcomers, formal language with no explanations, inaccessible minutes and a lack of breaks can easily be the norm. It is important to adapt structures to people with learning difficulties, rather than expect them to adapt to existing structures (for example, see box below).

A change for the better?

Simons (1997) provides a number of suggestions for ways of changing the meetings to make them more accessible. These include:

- becoming less formal (for example, not expecting everyone to address the meeting through the chair);
- incorporating breaks;
- making sure the purpose of each meeting is clearly explained;
- having all the papers for the meetings prepared in accessible formats (perhaps an audio tape), sent out well in advance;
- briefing people with learning difficulties before, and debriefing them after the meetings. People may well need time to work out what they want to say and how they are going to say it. They will also need to reflect and interpret what happened in the meetings;
- providing individual supporters whose prime role is to facilitate effective contributions from the individuals with learning difficulties;
- ensuring that items of interest to people with learning difficulties are not always at the bottom of the agenda;
- avoiding all jargon, and properly explaining all items.

Many of these steps can improve things for *everybody*.

Participation takes time

"Managers grossly underestimate the time it takes, and the complications, the personal problems and the institutionalisation faced by many people with learning difficulties."

(Advisor to self-advocacy group, quoted in Sutcliffe and Simons, 1993)

It takes time for people to learn new skills, or to get used to new arrangements or routines. The experience of suddenly being asked what they think, will not instantly counterbalance the weight of people's past experiences, which will have often given them the opposite message (keep your head down, don't make trouble).

Doing things participatively also takes time. For example, producing a set of accessible minutes will probably take longer than doing it in a conventional format, particularly if any audio-taping is involved. Similarly, the typical People First group may well only meet once a month and so any schedule must allow for the cycle of monthly meetings if consultation and feedback are required. These processes cannot be rushed.

Attitudes as risks and barriers

The range of commonly expressed attitudes which either hinders or distorts effective participation includes:

- Reluctance to raise expectations
Consciously or unconsciously, many services manage demand by rationing information about what is possible (see for example Ellis, 1993), often reflecting widespread concerns about generating 'unrealistic demands'. There is a curiously circular logic to this belief that expectations should not be raised, since it is frustrated expectations that fuel change.

- Tokenism, and fear of tokenism
There are plenty of examples of tokenistic participation - the 'business as usual' with a 'user-representative' present. Equally, although the fear of appearing to be tokenistic can be paralysing, some participation is better than no participation at all. Many initiatives will start being largely symbolic. However, as long as people learn from the experience and move on to improve their practice, that is not necessarily a problem.

- Wanting everyone to be involved
There has been a tendency in some services to look for a single solution that will balance all the conflicting concerns and pressures and (most importantly) that is completely inclusive:

"No, we decided not to do that, because we wanted to find a way to involve everyone."

(Manager in a day centre)

The trouble is, such a solution does not exist. Different ways of participating will be needed, all of which have different strengths and weaknesses. Waiting for the perfect mechanism that will work for everyone is a recipe for doing nothing.

The danger of subversion

Professionals who do not want things to change may subvert the process to their own ends - for example, by drawing users into a process to give a controversial decision some added legitimacy (*'Well they agreed to it ...'*). However, it is harder for professionals to subvert the process if there are some safeguards built in. These might include ensuring that individuals and groups understand the basis on which they are taking part, and have some tools to challenge professionals.

One way of ensuring that people with learning difficulties are not exploited is to negotiate some 'rules of engagement', which include the right for people with learning difficulties to withdraw their participation in protest. So, for example, Swindon People First have an agreement which sets out the terms on which they will join committees (see box below).

Swindon People First: an agreement to be on committees

The following is an excerpt from a contract which Swindon People First ask any organisation wishing to co-opt members of the group onto a committee to sign:

If you want People First to be on your committee you must agree these things to make it OK for us.

We should have a voice to say what we want.
You need to listen to us and give us time to talk.
We won't come to your committee just so it looks good.
You need to let us know why you want us on the committee.
You need to tell us what we will get out of being on your committee.
You have got to make minutes and agendas on tape if we want them.
If we need a supporter we will choose them.
The committee should pay for the supporter.
Everyone on the committee needs to be trained to know how to involve us.
The committee has to use words we understand.
We must be able to stop meetings if we need you to say something again or explain it.
Everyone should have their expenses paid and get the right amount.
If the rest of the committee get paid then we should too.

Consent and 'incapacity'

At some stage most services will have to deal with the issue of judging 'capacity' - the formal process for judging whether or not a person is legally able to enter into a binding contract of some form.

It is worth re-stating the current legal position here. As citizens, we have an inherent right to autonomy and self-determination. Currently, the common law assumes that every citizen is competent to make decisions for him or herself, and is therefore also responsible for the consequences of those decisions, unless proved otherwise (Roberts, 1997). This applies to people with learning difficulties as much as anybody else.

However, people with learning difficulties are likely to have assumptions made about their capacities, simply on the basis of their label. A good example is the continuing reluctance of the Charities Commission to accept people with learning difficulties as Trustees, even in the case of 'user-led' organisations like People First groups. While being a Trustee is a position of considerable responsibility, this reluctance is not based on any individual test of capacity to take on the role, but on a blanket assumption of incapacity.

These are important issues that commissioners and purchasers need to address directly, through ensuring that:

- services recognise and respect the rights of individuals to autonomy and self-determination;

- any test of capacity is not excessive, and that before incapacity is accepted, every effort is made to provide individuals with the skills and information they need to make informed decisions;

- no blanket assumptions of incapacity are made simply on the basis of a label;

- incapacity in one area of decision making is not a reason for either reducing opportunities for self-determination in other aspects of life, or for excluding people from participation.

Recognising the distinct role of carers

Participation also involves 'carers': families, friends and other 'informal' supporters. There are tensions around the development of 'user-participation', since the experience of many families over the years has led them to see their primary role as being to speak for their sons and daughters, or brothers and sisters with a learning difficulty. Many have been very effective in this role, showing great commitment over many years, and it is important that we do not suddenly devalue that contribution. However, some carers have perceived user-participation as a professional 'plot' to exclude themselves, and have resisted such developments.

When tensions arise due to differences in views between people with learning difficulties and their carers, it is important to recognise that carers too have a right to comment on services, often have an active role in supporting people with learning difficulties, and indeed may have their own needs for services, something the Carers (Recognition and Services) Act 1995 specifically recognises.

Despite certain tensions, users and carers may still have plenty in common. In some instances they have worked effectively together, occasionally forming coalitions. For either users or carers to achieve their goals, both will have to occasionally co-operate with each other. Helping them keep a separate identity, but also form a working relationship, is, therefore, a sensible strategy for commissioners.

Remember children exist

Most of the examples in this book focus on adults. Yet, in terms of participation, probably one of the most marginalised groups are *children* with learning difficulties.

As a matter of *principle* everybody - including children - should have their views taken into account as far as is humanly possible. Those interested in pursuing this issue should see the briefing paper by Linda Ward (1997) which discusses the Joseph Rowntree Foundation's programme of research and development concerning disabled children.

Chapter 3: A Responsive Framework?

The strategic elements of commissioning - developing a clear vision of how services should work and articulating that vision through strategic planning - have traditionally been high status activities carried out at some distance from the lives of people with learning difficulties. Yet setting the framework within which services will develop will involve making critical decisions that people with learning difficulties will want to influence.

This chapter begins to explore why participation needs to be considered as part of a strategic vision, and how participation events can offer opportunities for people with learning difficulties to influence the wider strategy.

Developing a strategy on participation

How can we ensure that services really address the issues that matter to people with learning difficulties? The following extract from the Greater Glasgow Joint Community Care plan gives an example of just some of the elements that might form a statement of principle on participation.

Extract from the *Greater Glasgow Joint Community Care Plan* for 1995

- people need to be *informed on a regular basis* and in ways that are easily understood in order to extend and improve awareness about community care;

- agreed avenues and forums should be established to encourage *meaningful consultation and participation;*

- opportunities for *representation, advocacy and campaigning* are essential to advance citizenship rights;

- the needs and views of carers and users must be a *major influencing factor in shaping community care services;*

- *positive action and commitment* is needed to empower community care clients, their carers or representatives and where appropriate community organisations, to directly participate in the planning and management of their own services and to express their views about the services they receive;

- there must be a *commitment to partnership* with local community and voluntary organisations as providers of services, involving the provision of advice, guidance and specialist help where this can establish and strengthen community control, ownership and management.

Getting started

It would probably be the ultimate paradox to develop a participation strategy, and not involve people with learning difficulties in the process. Quite clearly the first step has to be for commissioners and purchasers to begin developing some engagement with people who use services and their supporters.

Typically, the tactics for initiating the process include one or both of the following two actions:

1. carry out an audit of existing participation activities and user groups
It is more than likely that there will already be things going on, many of them driven by users or user-led groups. The worst possible start would be to establish an approach which, albeit unwittingly, sidelined these grass-roots initiatives.

2. hold a 'user conference'
Increasingly, services are starting to hold conferences specifically for users. There are a number of really good arguments for seeing this as a first step in developing a relationship. First, conferences are generally high status activities that staff get to go to, and from which users are, for the most part, excluded. Given the chance, many people with learning difficulties are keen to see what all the fuss is about. Many user conferences get a surprisingly high turnout.

Secondly, setting up a conference provides a good opportunity to begin working together with a local self-advocacy or People First group. It offers a very concrete set of objectives, with plenty of opportunities for responding positively to suggestions from people with learning difficulties.

Where there is no established local group, there is always the possibility of getting one of the more established user-led organisations from outside the area to play an important role in the conference, offering some positive role models for local users of the services. This is precisely the tactic adopted by MacIntyre Care, to great effect (see below).

Boss for a day

In 1993, the voluntary organisation MacIntyre Care celebrated the first United Nations day for disabled people by holding a workshop for people who used their services. The day was facilitated by some trainers with and without learning disabilities from the group Advocacy in Action, based in Nottingham. As well as talking about issues like 'labelling', 'speaking out', and 'things to be proud of', the workshop also included a session called *'If I were the boss ...'*. Each person in the workshop took a turn to say what he or she would do if they were the boss of MacIntyre Care. The answers ranged from the very specific *(more custard creams)* to the very general *(help old people)*. However, there was much to provide the management of MacIntyre Care with food for thought.

For example, the list of recommendations included:

- A job for everyone;
- Help to buy own home;
- Close the big houses. People should live in small houses;
- Help choose staff;
- The bosses should leave their offices and work in the house so they can find out what is really happening.

Eighteenth out of the 28 suggestions on the list was '*Read this list of recommendations*', which presumably the MacIntyre management did, because they issued a response, called '*The bosses talk back*'.

The documents are available from MacIntyre Care (see resource section).

To be successful, a conference has to be well organised. Attention needs to be paid to practical details. For example, provide plenty of opportunities for small group discussions and workshops; that means plenty of space in environments where the overspill of noise is not a problem. It can be difficult to find venues of any size that can effectively meet this requirement. Similarly, there are a lot of venues that claim to be accessible to people in wheelchairs that in practice turn out not to be. It does not make a good beginning to the day when the disabled person co-chairing the day cannot get up on the stage, or even into the hall!

The messages conveyed by the event are *important*, such as having people with learning difficulties and other disabled people play active leadership roles. Holding the event outside services in an attractive venue can significantly influence the tone of the day. While it might be useful for people like the director of social services to come and speak, it is also important that he or she is there to *listen* as well. There will need to be plenty of supporters to facilitate groups, and where possible they should be independent of the mainstream services.

Guidelines on involving service users and carers in local services

For those with access to the Internet, the National Institute for Social Work (NISW) and Surrey Social Service have published some guidelines on involving users and carers in local services on the NISW world wide web site (see resources section). These include specific suggestions on running participation events.

Meeting the bigwigs

*"How can you be a purchaser without knowing what you are
purchasing, to have been out and experienced it?"*

(McGowan, 1996)

Chandra McGowan works as a commissioner for West Surrey Health Authority
and was involved in a 'user-focused' review of services (described in the box
below). As part of this review she spent the best part of a week with one
particular service user, sharing as many aspects of her life as possible. The
experience led Chandra to a critical reappraisal of the quality of the services she
was purchasing (see McGowan, 1996).

Outcomes for people

In 1994, the National Development Team was commissioned by a group of
purchasers to carry out a series of reviews as part of the local long-stay
hospital resettlement programme. One of the aims of the reviews was to try
and ensure that people with learning difficulties were centrally involved.

A series of teams was recruited, which included two service users, family
members, senior managers on the purchasing side and staff working in the
services.

Where possible, the service users were supported partly by people recruited
specifically for the purpose, and partly by other members of the team.

Each member of a review team was matched with an individual with learning
difficulties using the service (the focus person), chosen to represent the full
range of disabilities and living arrangements in the service under review. The
teams were provided with two days training provided by the NDT consultants,
after which an extensive range of review visits were arranged. Each team
member made a series of visits to their focus person over a five day period,
including the weekend. The aim was for each team member to have a much
more rounded picture of what it was like to use that service.

After each series of visits, each member of the team provided a presentation
to the others about their focus person and their lives, and together the team
offered wider conclusions about the service. These points were then fed back
to the service providers. As Chandra McGowan recognises, this could often be
quite an uncomfortable experience. Sometimes the teams had expressed
considerable concerns about some aspects of the services. However, every
attempt was made to make the feedback as constructive as possible, and
Chandra readily acknowledges there were always good points which it was
possible to acknowledge and support. At the same time, having based the

conclusions on direct experience, it was harder for the services to challenge some of the less comfortable conclusions.

Having people with learning difficulties as part of the team was seen as a very positive development. According to the final report, they made a significant contribution to the exercise, but the experience of being part of the review was a difficult one for many of the team members (professionals, service users and families), and the importance of appropriate support is not to be underestimated.

A report of the review, called *Outcomes for People,* is available from Chandra McGowan at the West Surrey Health Authority.

Not all contact between the 'bosses' has to be formal. There is a good argument that everyone involved in purchasing and commissioning services should have regular opportunities to meet and get to know at least a few of the people who use the services for which they are responsible. As one of the quotes at the start of this book implies, there is also an issue about 'the bosses' being prepared to 'show their faces' in services.

Advocacy resources box

As well as following some of the references in this section, there are a number of other additional sources of information and advice on different forms of advocacy. These include:

Self-advocacy
London Boroughs People First publish a national newsletter, and can also help people identify local groups. Northampton People First have a web site, and are a useful source of contacts.

Information Exchange on Self-advocacy and Participation
Since 1991 Andrea Whittaker, a member of the Community Care Group at the King's Fund Centre, has been organising an informal information exchange around self-advocacy and user participation. The information distributed by the exchange is targeted particularly at the supporters and advisors of self-advocacy groups, along with other people who have a role in working in partnership with people who use services, ensuring they have a range of practical information and useful contacts.

Citizen Advocacy
Although its primary focus is on London and the South, Citizen Advocacy Information and Training (CAIT), may well be able to assist in pointing to resources and identifying the nearest citizen advocacy organisation.

Circles of Support
Circles Network is an organisation intended to promote and encourage the development of circles of support. As well as advice and contacts, they have published a handbook and video which sets out these ideas in a lot more detail.

Coalitions of Disabled People, Centres for Independent Living (CILs) and Personal Assistance Schemes
The British Council of Disabled People is the national umbrella organisation for organisations led by disabled people, and will be able to provide contacts of local coalitions of disabled people, along with a list of all CILs in the UK.

For those with an interest in personal assistance schemes, contact the National Centre for Independent Living.

The contact addresses and telephone numbers of all these organisations are included in the resource section.

Independent advocacy

In Chapter 2 we underlined the importance of advocacy, which is independent from service providers. Quite clearly, the responsibility for ensuring that independent advocacy is available to those who need it lies at the strategic level, in other words with commissioners.

Advocacy can mean many different things and there is a strong case for all of the following:

- independent People First groups;
- citizen advocacy, crisis or complaints advocacy, peer advocacy and circles of support;
- service brokerage;
- coalitions of disabled people.

We discuss each of these in more detail below.

Independent People First groups

"I see it as the job of the local authority, and the health authority, to help get such organisations off the ground and to nurture them."

(Roy Taylor, Chair of the Association of Directors of Social Services Disability Committee[1], talking of independent user-led advocacy organisations)

[1] Speaking at the 1997 Values Into Action *Funding Freedom* conference

Many services have 'self-advocacy groups', 'members' councils', 'users' committees' or 'users' forums' of various kinds. While these often have great value, there are inevitable limitations bound up with conflicts of interest, exclusion of non-members, identification with the service and inhibitions about voicing discontent. Some form of independent user group, such as People First, is therefore essential. The dilemma for services is that their own involvement in setting up an 'independent' group makes this very independence questionable.

The aim here should not be to impose but to inspire, and the first step is to make sure that people have information about such groups. There are videos now available, many of them made by people with learning difficulties themselves, which talk about their advocacy activities (for example see 'Start' in the resource section).

Putting users in touch with groups that might offer a role model is another important tactic. There are now a number of People First groups (along with organisations like Change and Advocacy in Action) who, for an appropriate fee, will come to conferences and explain what advocacy means to them, what they do, and how they work. Indeed, many groups will be supporting the development of local self-advocacy groups as part of their remit.

Once there is some interest and enthusiasm, it is much easier to avoid the danger of the whole initiative being professional-led. However, there is still plenty that services can do to help:

Assisting with Independent Facilitation
While professional help can be useful, most People First groups have found that *independent* facilitators have helped them become more effective. There has been much discussion of the role of facilitators, since there is a fine line between facilitating and taking over (see Dowson and Whittaker, 1993). When groups have the resources to employ their own supporters, the result can be a very different relationship between project workers and group members.

Resources
In the initial phases of development, provision of resources is crucial. For example, for groups to put in bids for other sources of funding, they must have access to the skills to develop business plans. In the case of Bristol and District People First, the Phoenix NHS Trust, along with Norah Fry Research Centre, provided £600 to pay for an independent consultant to help an existing People First group put in an effective bid for joint finance. This resulted in three years funding, enabling the group to establish an office and to employ a number of workers (including people with learning difficulties). Some 'seedcorn money' to help a group establish itself will also increase its chance of attracting subsequent funding from bodies like the Lottery Board or Charities Project, or will enable it to develop the skills and experience to do things that will themselves be income generating. It is important that funding comes with as few strings as possible.

Recognition and Support

Recognition and support includes ensuring that attendance at meetings is seen as a fundamental right for members, and that staff actively aid people to get there. It should also involve making sure the group has a critical role in the wider participation strategy.

Helping to Develop Leadership Skills

Like any new organisation, newly formed People First groups will have a lot to learn. Those most actively involved will need to develop leadership skills: from organising meetings, through to running an office and being a good employer. Purchasers and providers can help by providing appropriate training and advice.

Citizen advocacy, crisis or complaints advocacy, peer advocacy, and circles of support

Citizen advocacy is about the development of a supportive relationship between an unpaid private citizen (the advocate) and someone who is vulnerable or at risk of isolation. The aim of the relationship is to provide the latter with someone who is 'on my side', and whose role will be to help him or her achieve their goals (see Simons, 1993). Citizen advocates also represent a link into local communities.

Most citizen advocates are recruited by coordinators working for an independent organisation. Given the potential role of advocates in challenging services, citizen advocacy organisations often have an uneasy relationship with services, and the movement has set great store by trying to be as independent of services as possible. Nevertheless, some kind of funding from services is, in all probability, going to be critical in getting such groups established.

Citizen advocacy has always incorporated various forms of shorter-term *crisis advocacy*. With the development of complaints procedures, this has often developed into *complaints advocacy*. Complaining, particularly about a large bureaucracy which has a lot of control over one's life, is not easy. The official guidance on complaints in social services departments recognises this, and makes support for people who wish to make a complaint a mandatory requirement (SSI, 1991b). However, it does not specify what form this help should take, and many local authorities have not organised any independent support for people making complaints (Simons, 1995). Simons describes a number of initiatives around complaints procedures, including one citizen advocacy organisation which had been given additional resources to recruit advocates specifically to help people use the social services department's complaints procedure. Often these advocates would be recruited specifically for their experience and knowledge of the procedures, and unlike conventional citizen advocacy relationships, it was not unusual for the same advocate to work with a number of different people over time.

A second complaints advocacy scheme is *peer advocacy,* where people who had been supported to use the complaints procedure were later recruited and provided with training so that they could act as advocates themselves. It is not unknown for people with learning difficulties to act as very effective advocates for each other. Similarly, in some areas, complaints advocacy is actually offered by independent self-advocacy groups.

Finally, over recent years there has been increasing interest in the idea of *circles of support* (see Wertheimer, 1995). A circle of support is a group of people who agree to meet on a regular basis to help a vulnerable individual achieve their *own* goals. Members of a circle typically include friends, family, and other people from the local community who have got to know the person at the centre of the circle. Circles can and do include members of staff, but this is on the understanding that they are there because they know the person, and not as a professional. Similarly, many circles will also include other people with learning difficulties.

Service brokerage

By definition, both self-advocacy and citizen advocacy involve people who are not professionals. Yet there are times when people with learning difficulties need access to independent expertise. This is particularly the case when the services are not offering appropriate assistance and are unwilling to explore alternatives. While it is relatively easy for people with learning difficulties to say what is wrong, it is much harder for them to put forward the case for something different unless they have the necessary knowledge. It is at this point that a professional advocate might be needed: someone with the capacity to put together a proposal for an alternative service that would be viable.

Professional advocates are relatively rare and are usually found in service brokerage projects (see Brandon, 1994; Dowson, 1995). Service brokerage draws heavily on experiences in Canada. Back in the 1970s a group of families from Vancouver became very disillusioned with traditional services. They wanted a system that *started* with the interests of their sons and daughters, and which took account of the links between the person with learning difficulties, their family, and their community. Service brokerage was developed as a system for designing services which would reflect these aims.

Service brokers are (ideally) independent agents who are only accountable to disabled people (and their friends and family) who have chosen to seek their help. They help decide what kinds of support are needed, then design and negotiate a package of services from the most appropriate source. Service brokerage could play a critical role in developing change, particularly where local care managers may lack the specific knowledge and skills needed to develop more individualised services.

However, while there has been a lot of interest in service brokerage within the UK, there are as yet few genuinely independent service brokerage projects in existence (see Brandon, 1994). Where service brokers do exist (for example, in Southwark Consortium - see Dook et al, 1997) they are not strictly independent.

The reasons for this are not entirely clear, but they probably reflect a lack of access to individualised budgets. Now that the legislation on direct payments (see p. 37) has been passed, there may be increased demand for advocates to help individuals make best use of their cash.

Coalitions of disabled people

People with learning difficulties also have a role within the wider disability movement. Encouraging and supporting the involvement of people with learning difficulties in wider coalitions is an important role for commissioners. Indeed, thinking about participation beyond the narrow confines of 'client groups' may be a significant development in the future (see box below for an example).

POhWER

POhWER stands for 'People of Herts want equal rights'. It is an independent user-led advocacy organisation, in which people with learning difficulties play a significant role.

POhWER grew out of the Advocacy Development Project, an initiative established in 1992 by Hertforshire Social Services Department to try and stimulate good quality advocacy. According to Tim Anfiligof, the Advocacy Development Worker, it was always intended that this initiative would lead to the development of a broad-based, independent user-led organisation.

The project was based on a number of assumptions. These included:

- the need for generic advocacy

Although the project started with groups of users organised on client group lines, what emerged was the commonality of people's needs for support, something that was emphasised in the advocacy handbook that the project developed.

- the need to be inclusive

From the earliest stage, every effort was made to draw in as wide a range of service users as possible.

This led the project to think about how to establish an entirely independent agency. With funding from the Platinum Trust providing sessional training and other assistance, the 'People who use Advocacy Services' group was formed, made up of people with a wide range of labels. The result of their deliberations was the launch of POhWER in 1996.

People with learning difficulties were part of the driving force for the formation of POhWER, and are well integrated in its structure. For example, POhWER's constitution specifies that one of the Trustees must be someone with learning difficulties (places are also reserved for someone with physical disabilities, a deaf person, a blind person, an older person, someone who has used mental health services, and someone from an ethnic minority community who uses services). At the time of the launch, Richard Maylin from North Herts People First was acting as co-chair of the Trustees, and a further three Trustees also had a learning disability. A majority of the Trustees must be people who have experienced disability and discrimination. The structure of POhWER is designed to ensure that it:

- is genuinely independent, and is able to support advocacy schemes without conflict of interest. It must also be able to raise funds independently;

- is led by people with a wide range of disabilities;

- can act as a clearing house for advocacy issues across the county;

- provides an employment structure for local advocacy projects;

- will be able to support the development of new projects, providing a model of user-controlled management;

- promotes minimum standards among all affiliated advocacy organisations.

Perhaps the most striking feature of Hertfordshire is how an initiative that was effectively started by professionals has been able to build in steadily accumulating layers of participation, so that the final structure is very much the creation of disabled people.

Bringing the stakeholders together

In Chapter 2 we made the point that participation needs to enable people with learning difficulties to influence the wider system. Just to take one specific example, local housing policies can have a strong bearing on the kinds of opportunities that people with learning difficulties (particularly those that do not want to live in residential care) can access. For example, what priority are people with learning difficulties accorded on the housing list? Are there joint housing and social services assessments?

Commissioners also need to make sure that people with learning difficulties (and their families and supporters) have access to these critical stakeholders. This was just what was attempted in Oxfordshire (see box overleaf).

Getting together

In 1995, a joint strategy for learning disability services was published by Oxfordshire Health Authority and Oxfordshire Social Services Department. This document had been developed with the assistance of a large 'reference group' which included providers, families, and users of services, and a draft version had been the subject of an extensive consultation exercise. At the time of the publication the commissioners committed themselves to regularly reviewing the policy, and so in 1996 a one-day conference was duly organised to try and draw together all the various stakeholders (in particular, users and their families) and to look at how the strategy was working in practice.

A very wide range of individuals and groups were invited to the day, including representatives from the local housing department, local housing providers, social services managers, health purchasers, councillors, health providers, independent sector providers, GPs, advocacy organisations, the local colleges of further education, and of course users and families.

Prior to the conference, local user representatives got together and talked about the strategy, and met with the organisation 'Change', who were to open the conference. Change is a national organisation which focuses around people with learning difficulties who have a sensory loss. It employs people with learning difficulties, and ensures they play a leading role. The Change presentation involved taking some of the views from local users, along with Change's own experiences, and getting them across in the most accessible way possible through drama and role play, to explore the way professionals communicate, how it often feels to people with learning difficulties, and how it might be improved.

The rest of the morning was divided into workshops that represented different aspects of the strategy: access to the community, a place to live, personal support services, short-term break services, and personal development. The last of these was presented by two local advocacy organisations and was led by someone with learning difficulties.

The afternoon started with a presentation by the Director of Oxfordshire Social Services, which was followed by parallel streams of workshops. One stream was targeted at providers, and was designed to explore some of the key issues, including ideas around quality assurance. The second stream (called *What's next, what's missing?*) was specifically designed as an opportunity for users and families to express their views. Here, each small group was supplied with an outside facilitator and an 'illustrator': someone whose role was to make sure that the views expressed were recorded in an accessible way. The briefing notes for the facilitators were very clear:

> *If you have people who are not direct users or carers in the group, they will need to be there as observers, as the workshop is about gaining the views of users and carers, not professionals.*

The day ended with a feedback session from the groups, who were each asked to briefly describe the three main issues they had discussed.

Direct payments

Since April 1997, social services departments have had the power to provide disabled people with cash to pay for assistance. Potentially, these 'direct payments' offer disabled people one way of taking more control over their lives.

The Government's draft legislation originally suggested that people with learning difficulties should be excluded from direct payments. They are now included in the scope of the legislation but many people with learning difficulties still find it hard to access direct payments, largely because of the emphasis on the individual being a direct employer. Most people with learning difficulties are not seen as being able to take on this role because of the additional help they may require.

The legislation specifies that people must be able to consent to direct payments, and be able to manage their money, *with assistance* if necessary. Commissioners and purchasers will therefore need to give some thought to how best to support people with learning difficulties in their use of direct payments, whether through improving existing personal assistant schemes or by developing additional options. Frustration with existing arrangements has led at least one People First group to consider setting up their own personal assistance scheme. The report by Values Into Action (Holman and Collins, 1997), gives details of a number of relevant organisations, including the National Centre for Independent Living (see also the resources section) which provides advice, training and consultancy on setting up independent living schemes.

Understanding the system

Many user and carer groups have developed as a response to inadequacies of services. Their role has been to 'fight' the statutory agencies and campaign for better services, often with great determination, over the years. This can be a real difficulty where services are trying to respond to the wishes of people with learning difficulties but are meeting continuing resistance from carers organisations:

> "They [families] would probably say improve it, but don't change it ...
> For a long while their role has been in criticising the Council for lack
> of action: 'You've never delivered the goods'. However, they have not
> got out of the habit. It is difficult to engage people."
>
> (Local authority manager)

Many small groups lack the skills required to form the types of effective coalitions that can have such a significant influence on events. They may also lack the necessary understanding of how the system works. It was partly to address this problem that Knowsley Metropolitan Borough became a participant in *Partners in Policymaking*. The principle here was that genuine partnerships need to be based on equal access to both knowledge and skills.

Partners in policymaking

Partners in Policymaking is a leadership training programme for disabled people and parents of school age children. In 1996 the North West Training and Development Team (based at Calderdale), with support from the Home Farm Trust and the National Development Team, established the first course outside the US. Held over 16 days spread out over a total period of eight months, the course was attended by 29 individuals: 23 parents and six disabled adults.

The subjects tackled included:

- the history of services for disabled people;

- education, and in particular opportunities for access to mainstream schools;

- policy development: how decisions get made at a local and national level and how to influence them;

- advocacy, including developing alliances, community organising and promoting change.

Between sessions, participants were asked to carry out assignments, including writing to local MPs on an issue, visiting services, or commenting on local policies.

The range and depth of information presented, along with chances to try out and develop new skills, plus opportunities to network, provided a framework that was unparalleled in the UK, particularly for people who are not professionals. A brief evaluation of the first UK course is available through the North West Training and Development Team (NWTDT, 1996), which includes details of the programme. The course in the North West is to be repeated, and courses are being set up in the South of England, under the auspices of Circles Network UK (see resource section).

Strategic planning

Section 10 of the 1986 Disabled Persons Act requires local authorities to consult organisations of disabled people when co-opting onto strategic planning bodies. However, a review by Warburton (1990) for the Social Services Inspectorate found that this happened relatively rarely, and that there was still a widespread reliance on representatives from organisations *for* disabled people. It is a reasonable assumption that the direct presence of people with learning difficulties on such strategic planning bodies remains relatively rare. None were encountered in any of the visits or contacts made as part of this project, although there are some documented instances of it happening: for example, the planning mechanisms established as part of the All Wales Strategy (see box opposite).

Involvement of people with learning disabilities in formal structures: the All Wales Strategy

Unlike England, Wales has had a much greater involvement of central government (through the Welsh Office) in coordinating service provision. The All Wales Strategy has ensured a rather more consistent approach to planning and development in the Principality over the last decade with the involvement of both people with learning disabilities and their carers.

As Steve Beyer points out, this was not easy to achieve:

> *"The role of people with learning difficulties was said to have been slow to emerge and was seen as a failure of the early planning phases. This was more due to a failure to find effective ways to support their participation."*
>
> (Beyer, 1996)

Gradually things improved: effective relationships between the different groups were established, the lessons about the importance of accessible materials and personal support for people with learning difficulties were learnt. Although the extent of participation varies from county to county, there are now good examples of people with learning difficulties being firmly established in formal planning structures.

Bewley and Glendinning (1994) describe an anonymous authority whose county-level planning structure consists of a 'joint secretariat', which includes representatives of social services, health, education, voluntary organisations, families and People First groups. While the representatives of voluntary organisations and families were chosen through a county-wide voluntary sector forum, the people with learning difficulties were recruited through a parallel structure; all the local People First organisations (a county-wide coordinating group, plus six local groups) elect their own representatives.

Bewley and Glendinning identify three strengths of this particular system:

● long-term support and funding for local self-advocacy groups, enabling them to play a more effective role;

● a clear structure, with scope for different views to be articulated and assimilated;

● imaginative use of different methods of consultation to back up the structures.

Unfortunately, just at the point when the local systems were consolidating, there has been what is widely perceived to be a weakening of Welsh Office commitment to the Strategy. As the effects of the community care reforms, along with local government reorganisation, ripple through, many of the planning structures are being merged, leading to fears that the distinct voice of people with learning difficulties will be lost.

The demands of the wider system ensure that strategic planning bodies tend to be relatively formal, and will have a preponderance of professionals. This is always going to be a difficult environment for some people with learning disabilities. A rather different tack has been taken in Gloucestershire. Here a 'Shadow' strategy group has been established, specifically for people with learning difficulties. Although not officially part of the planning structure, this group has developed some influence (see box below).

Emerging from the shadow?

The Joint County Strategy Group (JCSG), the main strategic planning body locally, had wanted to develop some user representation. One user of the county's learning disability services was co-opted, and was provided with a supporter. It soon became clear that one person was not going to successfully represent all the different interests of people with learning disabilities in Gloucestershire, and so the 'Shadow County Joint Planning Group' was formed.

The Shadow Group has a direct semi-formal relationship with the JCSG, such as exchange of minutes. It initially came quite low on the JCSG's priorities, but gradually the messages from users are working their way up the agenda. The Shadow Group has about twenty members and has been responsible for deciding how representatives are selected. The group also has an independent facilitator.

Efforts have been made to encourage people to report back to their constituencies and act as effective representatives. Minutes of the meeting are available with pictures and symbols, and are also available on tape. Members have been provided with questions designed to help them elicit their fellow users' views about specific issues. The group also keeps in contact with local self-advocacy groups.

In her role as the Joint Learning Disabilities Development Officer, Jane Raha regularly attends the group, as does a local occupational therapist who is involved in a local quality action group initiative. Senior managers and other significant figures also attend meetings, either at their own request or responding to an invitation from the group.

It has not always been easy for the JCSG and the Shadow Group to respond to each other. On the whole, Jane feels most of the issues actively raised by the Shadow Group members are 'immediate' rather than 'strategic', and have often been quite difficult for the JCSG to deal with. It has taken time for the Shadow Group to learn the necessary skills and become established. Resources have been scant, and so far it has not been possible to offer some of the training that Jane feels would be of benefit to people in this new role.

However, the group has steadily evolved, and the people with learning difficulties have felt able to ask the really basic questions (*'What is that for?'*) that others have either taken for granted or have perhaps been too intimidated to query. The members have become particularly interested in the ways that elected Members (on the Council) make decisions.

There is some danger that a 'Shadow Group' will always remain marginalised, since the opportunities for direct relationships with other stakeholders in the strategic planning process are limited. However, being outside the formal system has its advantages. Gloucestershire has seen extensive protests against cuts in services by disabled people, and an advantage of the Shadow Group structure is that its members have been able to join in without any inhibitions. It is not bound by any collective responsibility, since it is not jointly responsible for the decisions. As Bewley and Glendinning (1994) point out, many groups of disabled people are beginning to discover that staying outside the system and being free to campaign can, in some circumstances, be as effective as having formal status. Also, unlike the earlier attempts to co-opt a representative onto the JCSG, the Shadow Group has offered a space for people to develop their own voice at their own pace.

Community care plans

Local authority social services departments are now required to publish community care plans on an annual basis. They are meant to consult widely on these plans, particularly with users of services, and with user-led organisations. Many rely on public meetings, but people with learning difficulties are often marginalised within this process. Recognising this, some areas have paid particular attention to working with existing self-advocacy groups:

> *"We should talk to people in their own space, at their own pace, with known supporters."*

> (Social Services Manager)

Information on participation in community care planning

Consulting people with learning difficulties about community care plans is one of the areas that has been tackled by the information exchange on self-advocacy, and user participation established by the King's Fund (see advocacy resources box earlier in this chapter). The findings from their brief survey (April 1995) reveal a range of different experiences of the consultation process, from the distinctly negative ('much anger all round' was one comment) to the distinctly positive. There were instances where people with learning difficulties had a genuine chance to comment and where their ideas and suggestions were subsequently incorporated into the final plans. For example, one member of a self-advocacy group argued for a telephone helpline for people who were living independently, and this suggestion duly appeared in the local Action Plan. There were a number of signs that some authorities at least were taking the process seriously, organising conferences and bringing in outside facilitators.

Often there were positive spin offs from the process, such as an opportunity for senior managers and people with learning difficulties to get to know each other 'face to face'.

For many of those providing the material for the information exchange, this was the first serious attempt to consult people with learning difficulties about community care plans. Andrea Whittaker, the editor of the information exchange, suggests the following four key points to aim for:

1. a service culture which fosters ongoing involvement so that people can learn the necessary skills and become familiar with the processes over time;

2. enough notice of events to give people time to prepare properly (there were stories of people only getting the consultation documents the day before meetings);

3. documents 'translated' into a form that users can understand and work with;

4. adequate time built in for facilitators to support people.

Users of services also need to be included in the process of *developing* community care plans. Bewley and Glendinning (1994), found that only 12 per cent of local authorities reported having carried out *any* consultation before writing a draft of their first plan, effectively precluding the chance for disabled people to help set the overall agenda. Further, *very few* of the final plans indicated where changes had been made as a result of consultation on a draft.

As part of the process of developing a medium-term strategy, Hackney Social Services carried out a review of their own day and residential provision for people with learning difficulties (see opposite). Consultation on earlier community care plans, along with feedback from joint planning forums in which users had been involved, had highlighted some areas of dissatisfaction. The aim of the review was to identify these areas of concern, along with the features that people with learning difficulties and their families would classify as a 'good' service.

Feeding into the development of community care plans

Hackney Social Services established four 'focus' groups, comprising five or six users, three or four carers and two or three members of staff, including colleagues from other agencies. These groups were facilitated by social work staff. Each group met a number of times, carried out visits to local services, and produced their own reports. These reports were then used to develop the overall strategy. In an attempt to set the groups in a wider context, discussions were also held with London Boroughs People First, along with the National Development Team, who had been involved in carrying out an evaluation of one of Hackney's hostels.

Based on the information from this process, Hackney proposed to start developing a much wider range of accommodation alternatives, including some individualised supported living arrangements (see Kinsella, 1993; Simons and Ward, 1997).

The resulting report continued to foresee the involvement of all the potential stakeholders in services:

> "Many people were involved in the review. The 'next steps' must start with them ... a series of meetings will be set up to discuss the content of this report and to hear people's views about the practical issues and concerns that must be addressed during the planning stages. Getting people's views, though, is not enough. It is important that the people who have a stake in the service are involved in the planning of its future. So users, carers, staff and people from other agencies will be invited and encouraged to be involved in project teams which will do the detailed planning."

(Extract from *A new sense of direction*, Hackney Social Services, 1995)

Consultation involves the production of accessible versions of plans. A good example emerged from Glasgow, where the Joint Planning Team collaborated with *Project Ability*, a centre for developmental arts, to produce an accessible summary of the Joint Learning Disability Strategy, called *Choices for the Future*.

Choices for the future

The text is very simple and straightforward, with each point illustrated not with a drawing or a symbol but with a good quality colour photograph, showing real people in real places. A section at the front introduces the idea of the joint planning team, and explains what is meant by 'services'. Each subsequent section (for example 'somewhere to live', 'something meaningful to do') is then divided into two parts: one which shows things as they are now, and one with how things might be. These offer some very concrete examples of the future range of choices. They include a very clear commitment to enabling people to choose where and with whom they live, including on their own (with support if they need it).

After the release and distribution of the document, the planning team visited a range of day centres, hostels, group homes, adult education classes and Lennox Castle Hospital. Although *Choices for the Future* was just about as accessible as material in print can be, not all the hospital residents understood it. People in this group are now being paired with individual advocates, and are being shown some of the places they might live, as a way of helping them say or show what they want.

One of the strengths of the Glasgow document is the very clear statements contained within it:

> *In the future ... People will be able to choose who they would like to live with ...*

> *In the future ... There will be more support in local areas.*

Some developments will be dependent on additional funding and there is obviously going to be tension between accessibility - saying things very strongly and clearly - and informing people about the often complex realities of the political process involved in developing services. Glasgow's statements are bold, effectively giving the message that this is how things *ought* to be - challenge us if they are not.

Chapter 4: Putting it into Practice: Operational Planning and Purchasing

This chapter is concerned with the development of participation in operational planning and purchasing of services, and illustrates opportunities for participation in the more practical phases of the commissioning cycle.

Operational/locality planning

Most authorities will have some process for converting a broad strategy into operational plans at a local level - often described as locality planning. While the involvement of people with learning difficulties in strategic planning is relatively rare, some degree of participation in locality planning is more common. The following example (see box below) is from Hertfordshire.

Locality planning in Hertfordshire

In Hertfordshire, locality planning comprises three basic elements combined in different ways:

1. planning groups, usually with a long-term membership, which meet in a fixed cycle;

2. time limited project groups;

3. coordination of input from a network of groups.

These processes are further underpinned by various quality assurance groups monitoring standards and ways of improving services - in which both users and carers would be involved to varying degrees, along with service audits in which users are interviewed.

The precise form taken by local planning meetings has been deliberately left to local discretion. However, there is a clear expectation that users and carers will be involved, along with officers from social services and elected members.

According to Tim Anfiligof, who has been involved in supporting the local advocacy developments, the contact with both officers and elected members has resulted in big changes of attitude amongst both:

"There has always been political support for the Social Services Department, but in the past it was a case of doing for. Now there is much more interest in doing with. Through the contact in the locality, planning members in particular have discovered that users are fundamentally the same as them."

There have been difficulties. Tim feels at times that people's expectations of what can be changed can be very unrealistic. However, *because* they have now been involved over a reasonable period, people who use the services are getting a better sense of what can be done locally.

There is recognition locally that there is still a lot to be learnt. This is reflected in some of the suggestions to emerge from the locality planning process, including:

- producing a best practice guide on how to involve users and carers;

- requesting more resources to support user involvement, including sign language interpreters, transport, etc.;

- having an annual users' conference;

- mounting regular stakeholder conferences at county level on different issues;

- producing a training/skills development plan for agency staff involved in locality planning, focusing in particular on the effective involvement of users.

Accessible information

The need for accessible information might seem obvious, but its lack continues to plague services. Therefore, operational planning *will* have to address this issue.

The issues surrounding accessible information have become surprisingly controversial, with at least two distinct schools of thought. There is agreement that written material should have a combination of simple text, along with pictures and/or symbols; the question is, how should these be integrated? Many of the user-led organisations have adopted a relatively informal style: short, pithy sentences accompanied by a graphic. Although these will include symbols, they tend to be used in a representational (rather than strictly symbolic) style, and the graphic is usually an illustrative line drawing. The reader is able to roughly guess the meaning of the graphic without any prior training. Material produced by London Boroughs People First[1] and Change[2] mostly fits this mould.

---

[1]   Their booklet *Oi! it's my assessment* is a good example

[2]   Change were commissioned to produce an accessible version of the Mental Health Foundation's Committee of Inquiry into services for people with learning disabilities.

In contrast, much of the accessible information produced by professionals contains more emphasis on formal symbol systems, Makaton in particular. This tends to result in a style in which text is translated into symbols more or less word for word.

So what I user

There are variations on these themes. There are some user-led groups which have stuck to the formal symbols. Equally, in Somerset, where the emphasis is on 'total communication' (supporting people in their use of a whole range of communication styles in a way that suits the individual) and where there is extensive translation of text into symbols, there has also been a marked shift away from using the universally agreed Makaton standard. Indeed, local people with learning difficulties have been encouraged to get involved in developing their own symbols. If this provides less universality, it does promote a greater ownership on the part of people with learning difficulties.

The reservations expressed about the more informal approach centre on this inconsistent use of symbols. Certainly, any person with learning difficulties who had been trained to use Makaton symbols *could* be confused by the way some symbols get used interchangeably. Different people may not necessarily understand the same thing by any given graphic. Relatively few people actually seem to understand the Makaton symbols, and without prior training they can be difficult to interpret. Moreover, Makaton only provides a very limited set of symbols, designed to reflect 'basic' needs. Many important issues for participation are not covered. The direct translation of text also tends to make documents much longer (in itself a barrier to accessibility).

As yet, we really do not know enough about the relative effectiveness of the different approaches to make any definitive judgement about which is the more successful, particularly in the context of the 'real world', where the proportion of people (with and without learning difficulties) who are experienced users of Makaton varies considerably.

No information, no matter how it is formatted, will be accessible to everyone with learning difficulties. Most attempts to make information accessible rely on supporters to help explain the material. However, this is in itself a big step forward from the past, and a more accessible version of information often provides supporters with a tool to work with, rather than leaving them to do all the hard work.

Many groups augment written material with audio-tapes or, more rarely, videos, particularly for people with a hearing impairment who use Makaton or British Sign Language (BSL). Software has been developed which has made producing symbols-based materials much easier and the next few years will probably see people starting to explore the possibilities offered by multimedia computers to integrate sound, text, graphics and video in interactive formats. *The virtual tenancy* developed jointly by Metropolitan Housing Trust and Notting Hill Housing Trust (available from Pavilion Publishing) is just such an example.

Plain facts

Any accessible information strategy should open up as wide a range of information as possible. This was very much the thinking adopted at the Norah Fry Research Centre in an attempt to stop seeing people with learning difficulties simply as a focus for research, but also as potential users of the results.

In 1996, the Joseph Rowntree Foundation commissioned researchers at the Centre to replicate their *Findings* (the official summary the Foundation publishes for most of the work it supports) in an accessible format, targeted specifically at people with learning difficulties and their supporters. The result was a series of short accessible briefings called *Plain Facts*.

These are very short, with plenty of graphics, and very clear language, backed up with an audio-tape. The aim is both to provide a limited amount of focused information, and to inspire people to try and find out more. Therefore many of the *Plain Facts* contain suggestions for things that groups or individuals might try next.

Subjects covered include:
- housing and support options;
- living with another family (adult placements);
- making complaints;
- closing the last hospitals;
- supported employment;
- college and adult education;
- choosing staff;
- fair shares for all.

Plain Facts comes out roughly six times a year and is available free to self-advocacy groups and day services. A short report on the use of the initial eight issues, along with back copies of *Plain Facts* and advice on drafting a *Plain Facts* is available from the Norah Fry Research centre (see resource section).

Everyone has to take responsibility for ensuring that material going to people with learning difficulties is accessible and accommodates the skills and abilities of the recipients. However, it is not enough to leave the production of good accessible material up to individuals; there needs to be a coordinated strategy which includes:

- designated resources like desk-top publishing facilities and scanners;

- people with the skills and experience to use them effectively.

For material to be genuinely accessible, people with learning difficulties need to be actively involved in developing and testing it. One possible model for this kind of strategic support is the Bristol based information service Connect (see box below).

Connecting people with information

Connect is a joint-funded information and resources service, based in and managed through the Phoenix NHS Trust. The resource base has materials relating to services which are available to people with learning difficulties, their families and supporters, and professionals.

As well as providing conventional information, Connect has built up considerable expertise in developing and producing good quality accessible information. It has been involved in a wide range of tasks locally, including developing an easy-to-understand complaints leaflet, information for people with learning difficulties on individual planning, and an accessible version of the local community care plans.

Connect also produces BUZZ magazine. This award winning publication is produced for local people with learning difficulties *by* people with learning difficulties. Connect has a network of 25 'reporters' locally who provide material.

Encouraging user-led training and consultancy

In 1994, the Notting Hill Housing Trust established an initiative to promote tenant participation in their supported housing. After an initial tenants survey, there followed a programme of user-led training and consultancy. Some of that work was undertaken by Advocacy in Action. Further details of the initiative are included in *Whose Home is This?* (Simons, 1997).

Many positive strengths emerged with user-led training, and Advocacy in Action has won national awards for its work, which draws strongly on members' direct experiences of services. After all, people with learning difficulties are the 'experts' at being on the receiving end of services; they can deal with issues in ways that professionals cannot. For example, any workshop on labelling will not be an abstract affair; members of Advocacy in Action can talk about the actual names they have been called, and the terms used to describe them. Further, the involvement of people with learning difficulties in what is traditionally a role reserved for high status professionals sends very strong messages both to other users and to staff.

Advocacy in Action is not the only organisation to do this form of work: Skills for People (Newcastle), Change (London) and a number of People First groups across the country have all developed expertise in this area. These developments are likely to continue. Change and the National Institute of Adult Continuing Education (NIACE) have jointly developed a training pack designed to help people with learning difficulties develop the skills needed to become effective trainers. The pack can be used to deliver a course which is accredited through the Open College Network, and which would be eligible for funding through the Further Education Funding Councils. Further information is available through NIACE (see resource section).

It is worth adding a note of caution here. Like any other organisations, those run by disabled people will vary in their efficiency and their capacity to keep commitments. In one of the authorities visited by the author, a self-advocacy group had been commissioned to provide support to help develop other local groups, but their involvement appeared to have tailed off, and they were failing to respond to queries about the progress of the work.

The fact that user groups sometimes over-commit themselves is not surprising (indeed it will often reflect the pressures placed on them by agencies). However, where groups are being paid for their service, these difficulties pose a real problem.

Although many user-led groups are very good at what they do (in this sense they can be very professional) and would resent 'allowances' being made, at the same time they are often employed precisely because they are users and not 'professionals'. It is, therefore, important not to have unrealistic expectations of what user consultants can achieve; their involvement ought to be seen as a partnership to be fostered and supported by the agency. Suggestions for good practice include:

- the brief for their involvement needs to contain clear goals and should be developed *with* the consultants, rather than simply imposed upon them;

- there should be named individuals who will liaise with the consultants and who retain a degree of direct involvement in their work, allowing progress to be monitored;

- there should be regular opportunities for the consultants to meet with a steering group;

- there should be appropriate practical assistance to ensure that the user consultants concentrate their energy on the most important aspects of their work;

- the agreement should specify what would happen if things do not go to plan.

Selecting providers

The technical process of tendering might appear to offer relatively few opportunities for people with learning difficulties to participate. However, ensuring that tenders reflect the importance of participation could open up new opportunities.

One option for doing this is the 'pre-tender' meeting used by Staffordshire Social Services Department (see box below).

Participation in pre-tendering processes

The contracting section in Staffordshire Social Services Department was keen to start involving users and carers in the tendering process. It therefore decided to adapt the pre-tender meeting it has traditionally established for potential providers to ensure that users and carers have an active presence. This was done by turning the meeting into an event that was compared to a 'careers evening'. Each of the following had a 'table':

- the local care managers;
- the commissioners and the legal department;
- service users and carers.

The meeting was open to all potential providers, who were encouraged to attend and explore what the different groups would want from a service.

While it is important that the process for selecting providers is fair and consistent, this need not preclude the participation of people with learning difficulties.

Involving people in selecting providers

In January 1995, the contract for providing a local day service to 25 people with learning difficulties came to an end. The purchasers (Avon Health Authority) and the existing service providers worked together to design accessible selection criteria for the tender, which involved people with learning difficulties in the whole process.

The tender selection panel was established, consisting of a representative from the local People First group with a supporter, four users of the day services with their own independent supporters, two other stakeholders, and the Chief Executive and Contract Manager of the Health Commission.

The process started with each tendering organisation being invited to tender

---

by making a 15 minute presentation to the panel. The presentation had to be accessible and relevant. Instant photographs were taken at this stage to help orientate the panel later as to who represented each organisation.

In the afternoon, each organisation ran a practical 'taster' workshop for each panel member to try out its service. Selection was aided in a range of ways such as colour coding, a set of numbers and faces showing emotional response to the workshops, enthusiasm, boredom, etc. Eventually, agreement was reached amongst the panel, with a high degree of similarity between all the marks.

Lessons from the process

Pete Le Grys (from the Phoenix NHS Trust) identified a number of features which he feels contributed to the success of the project:

- the purchasers had a clear commitment to the process and had a clear understanding of the scoring system used;

- the involvement of facilitators and general support from non-panel people helped things run smoothly;

- the venue was in a community centre well known to all the service users;

- service users were well prepared, with three pre-selection briefings concentrating on 'being fair', 'how the day would run' and 'things they were looking for';

- the use of instant photographs and colour coding helped considerably;

- it was a long day, so supplies of tea, coffee, squash, biscuits and pre-prepared lunches were essential.

For further information contact Pete Le Grys at the Phoenix NHS Trust (see resource section).

Promoting participation among providers through contracting

As well as involving people with learning difficulties directly in their own activities, an important role for purchasers lies in promoting participation among service providers. In this section we look at ways in which purchasers can try to ensure that providers take participation seriously.

1. Involvement in contracting
The key to the formal relationship between purchasers and providers is the service contract. Crudely, these can be divided into two forms:

- spot contract
  A service is purchased on a one-off basis for a named individual.

- block contracts
  Here purchasers arrange a specific volume of services (e.g. so many places in residential care) without reference to individuals.

One way for services to ensure that the wishes of individuals are genuinely kept at the centre of the services is to develop individualised packages using 'spot purchasing', where the particular concerns of the individual can be built into the contract specifications. There is scope here for encouraging individual users to help write this element of the contract.

Even with the more traditional block contract, which for many years has been the norm in long-stay hospitals, there is still scope for building in clear details of how users might be involved. These might include:

- the need for a detailed participation strategy to be reviewed and monitored;

- clear guidelines about the nature of complaints procedures to be operated by the provider, with clear links to the purchaser's own procedures (see section on complaints procedures in Chapter 5);

- mechanisms for the goals jointly agreed by users, care managers and providers as part of any individual planning, to be incorporated as part of the wider service specification and monitored for progress.

The Advocacy Promotion Group

Advocacy Promotion was set up in Cardiff to help services (and others) listen to and act on the views and wishes of people with learning disabilities and their advocates. Members include representatives from People First, service providers, advocacy organisations and carers.

The group began by undertaking a small piece of research into how local services were trying to find out the views of their users, managing complaints procedures, training staff on advocacy and recognising when access to independent advocacy was necessary. They found that work in these areas was generally patchy. While there were examples of good practice locally, many services were missing out on opportunities to respond to the wishes and priorities of their users.

Their report gives recommendations and a checklist of good practice for services. The Joint Commissioning Group has subsequently agreed that these recommendations will be included in service contract specifications, so that all services will be expected to put into place mechanisms to ensure that the views of users are taken seriously. The Joint Commissioning Group will also be offering advice to services to assist them in developing these mechanisms.

The group now plans to continue its work promoting the importance of self-advocacy and other forms of advocacy with families and non-professionals.

Further details can be obtained from People First Cardiff and the Vale (see resource section).

2. Involving people with learning difficulties in appointing staff
Recruiting the right staff can make a big difference to the quality of people's lives. But who should decide who the 'right' staff are? Clearly, purchasers and providers will have their requirements in terms of qualifications and experience, but there is a good case for ensuring that people who use the service should also have a say in who is appointed.

Many services have been experimenting with the informal involvement of users for some time, but participation in formal processes like short-listing and interviewing is still rare (Townsley and Macadam, 1996). Lack of equal opportunities training is one of the most commonly cited reasons for not involving users. As a result, a training pack has now been specifically designed to deliver appointment-focused equal opportunities training to people with learning difficulties. *Getting involved in choosing staff* (Townsley et al, 1997) is available from Pavilion Publishing (see resource section). Purchasers could disseminate information about this or similar tools among providers.

3. Individual planning and care management
Since the early years of the 'ordinary life' movement, there has been an acceptance of the principle that services ought to be planned around each person, and that he or she (and their family) ought to be centrally involved in that process. Indeed, many hoped that individual planning would be the catalyst to drive services forward. The reality has not been so encouraging. While many services *are* much more responsive than in the past, individual planning has not, on the whole, delivered the changes that many hoped for (see, for example, Felce, 1996).

The reasons for this are complex, but at least in part reflect a confusion about the respective roles of purchasers and providers. In essence, the key question is how individual planning relates to the wider process of developing services. Many service providers see individual planning as part of their role, effectively using it to try and adapt the service to the individuals involved, often with little reference to care management. However, if individual planning is about service *design* (see box on person-centred planning below) then it needs to be very clearly linked to the care management process.

Person-centred planning and individualised services

If services are going to be more 'individualised' and responsive, ways will have to be found for involving people with learning difficulties in their design. This is certainly the case with 'supported living options' (enabling a person to live in his or her *own* home, with appropriate support - see Kinsella, 1993; Simons and Ward, 1997), which rely on detailed individual planning for their success. They have become widely associated with 'person-centred' approaches to designing services, the most commonly used version of which is 'essential lifestyles planning'.

Essential lifestyles planning begins with the premise that for each individual there will be a set of 'non-negotiables': key features of any service that *must* be in place for the service to work. The list of non-negotiables is developed in partnership with the individual and his or her family or supporters and is then used as a basis for specifying the service that will be needed. The process also looks for features that would be 'highly desirable' (elements of the service that ought to be in place, but which, at a pinch, the person could manage without) and 'desirable' (features which the person would like, but are less critical).

In Manchester, Helen Sanderson has been working with People First to explore some of these person-centred approaches, and her report (Sanderson et al, 1997) is available from Scottish Human Services.

By definition, person-centred approaches are meant to be participative; the individual with learning difficulties *has* to be at the centre of the process. Even for people without conventional ways of communicating, 'listening' to their behaviour will be a key to the process. By spending time with the person, and really getting to know them, by talking to people who know them well, by seeing people in different contexts, it *is* possible to build up a picture of the issues that are non-negotiable for them.

As people experience new situations and opportunities, their wishes and needs will inevitably change. Further, for people with complex needs (particularly those for whom the non-negotiables may be difficult to establish), an initial person-centred plan is likely to be an approximation. By implication, therefore, person-centred planning has to be a continuing and flexible process, with correspondingly flexible services. Clearly, *both* purchasers and providers will have a significant stake in the process.

These considerations raise significant dilemmas about who should be involved in producing detailed plans for individuals. Where people have more complex needs, this is likely to be a complex, time-consuming process; for care managers with a large generic caseload, person-centred planning may seem like an unaffordable luxury. On the other hand, while service providers may be in a better position to work intensively with individuals, they are not in control of resources, and they often face considerable conflicts of interest (the end result might be a design for a type of service that the provider does not offer, or has no experience of providing).

For a few areas, the way out of this impasse has been investment in more intensive specialist care management: ensuring that there are care managers with both the time and the experience to work *with* people, and then developing service packages (see Simons and Ward, 1997 for an example). Others have solved the dilemma by forging partnerships. In some cases this might involve providing specific resources to enable the most appropriate person to do the work (whether this is a provider, or even a service broker - see Chapter 3). In others, it has involved innovative collaboration between authorities and agencies. For example, Simons and Ward (1997) describe the situation in Liverpool, where the expertise of specialists within the North Mersey Health Trust is used to develop and establish supported living arrangements for people with the most complex needs (here, supported living is effectively being used as an alternative to a medium secure unit). Once stabilised, these arrangements are then passed to an independent agency. The transition is made possible by the secondment of staff from the independent agency to work with the specialists in the Trust through the person-centred planning and implementation phases.

Finally, quite apart from detailed individual planning, the introduction of care management has resulted in the adoption of an initial assessment process as part of the 'gateway' to services. However, many of the assessment forms used by services in this context are inaccessible, which both hampers participation and minimises the possibility of people with learning difficulties doing self-assessments.

This was an issue of concern in Knowlsey, where a pilot project has been established to try and improve the situation. At the time of the visit, some 40 people had been re-assessed using an experimental form in a more accessible format. The material on assessment produced by London People First (appropriately called *Oi! it's my assessment*) has also been used locally as a way of opening up the process to users.

Involving people in their own person-centred planning process is not the only way to introduce participation. For example, Simons (1997) describes how one particular housing and support organisation recruited one of their tenants with learning difficulties to help design the material the agency used to promote lifestyles planning, and was subsequently involved in the delivery of training to staff.

Chapter 5: How Well is it Working? Participation in Monitoring and Reviewing Services

Monitoring and reviewing services represent the final phase of the commissioning cycle. Equally, they form the basis for the turn of the cycle; the lessons learnt from monitoring and reviewing services can have a big influence on future developments. This chapter explores ways of involving people with learning difficulties in this process.

Provide a clear statement of users' rights and entitlements

One way to begin involving people with learning difficulties in monitoring and reviewing services is to provide some clear statement about their rights, and what they should expect from services. This will help create a climate in which users and their supporters know when and how to challenge services. For example, a statement confirming that certain forms of restraint are unacceptable could be a very useful tool for both users and their advocates. There have been some good examples of such documents. Simons (1993) provides some recommendations which draw on two documents from MacIntyre Care and Southwark Consortium, brief extracts from which are included in the box below. Other examples include material on sexual rights (Cambridge, 1996; McCarthy and Cambridge, 1996).

Charters: a case for some clear statements

An effective charter needs to make some very clear statements in a whole range of areas. These might include:

● a general statement of rights
For example, to form relationships of choice, to freely associate with others, to use their private property as they wish.

● specific rights in relation to advocacy
This might include the right to appoint an advocate, the right for that advocate to attend any meeting involving the person with learning difficulty and to be able to visit him or her at their place of residence. The right to join a self-advocacy group should also be explicitly recognised.

● the right to informed consent
People should have the right to any information they need to make informed decisions. Where people are not able to make an informed decision

---

themselves, there should be a very clear process for any substitute decision making, preferably giving full recognition to the role of family, friends and advocates.

- statements of specific entitlements

While it is difficult to be exhaustive, there should be some clear statements of what services are about. These should set the overall priorities (for example, explaining that services should help people to live as independently as possible) and should include some specifics (for example: 'if you do not get on with your key worker you can ask for a change').

- statements about what services will not do

If people are going to challenge what services do, then information about what is unacceptable practice can be very useful. So, for example, statements which explicitly outlaw any of the following would send a clear message to everyone involved: corporal punishment; material, sensory or psychological deprivation; collective sanctions; the use of seclusion; restriction of contact with friends, relatives or advocates as either a punishment or a tool to control behaviour.

- statements about how people can participate

Telling people that they have a right to be heard and that their views will be taken seriously is an important message.

Quality is our business too: outcome measures

Any monitoring process requires standards against which to judge services. There is a general consensus that these standards ought to focus in particular on 'outcomes' (what actually happens to people with learning difficulties) rather than 'processes' or 'inputs'. However, defining reliable outcome measures has never been easy, nor have existing measures always focused on issues that people with learning difficulties would necessarily see as a priority.

The Quality Network is a joint project between the British Institute of Learning Disabilities, the National Development Team, and the Oxfordshire Learning Disability NHS Trust, which has set out to improve the situation. The aim is to create a national accreditation project.

People with learning difficulties will be directly involved in two aspects of The Quality Network. These are:

1. a person-centred review process
Participating services will set up review teams (paralleling those described in Chapter 3) to bring together purchasers, senior managers, people with learning difficulties and families.

2. the use of outcome measures based on the views of, among others, people with learning difficulties

These measures will include an outcome statement, real life stories to illustrate ways in which people have managed to achieve the outcome, a summary in accessible language, examples of the evidence that would show whether the outcome has been achieved or not, guidance on practice that might be helpful (or a hindrance), evidence sheets, and a rating scale to be used in any review.

These measures cover the following areas:

- I make choices about my daily lifestyle;
- I make decisions about my life;
- I take part in everyday activities or get help to do this if I need it;
- people listen to me and treat me with respect;
- I have friendships and relationships;
- I participate alongside ordinary membership of the community;
- I get the chance to do a paid job and the help I need to do it well;
- I am safe from harassment and abuse;
- I make plans for the future;
- my family and I have a say in the services I receive.

Further information about the project is available from The Quality Network, c/o The Oxfordshire Learning Disabilities NHS Trust (see resource section).

Monitoring and evaluating services

We need to make sure that services are working as intended, both to protect people with learning difficulties and to ensure that scarce resources are being used properly. Commissioners *could* involve people with learning disabilities in helping them perform this task.

There are numerous examples of people with learning difficulties being involved in formally evaluating services, sometimes as part of a wider team. For example, the Social Services Inspectorate included people with learning difficulties in their inspection teams when they carried out a review of the use of leisure facilities in day services during 1994 (See SSI, 1995). Indeed, with the aid of facilitation from Peter Dawson of the East Midlands Further Education Council (see resource section), the Social Service Inspectorate involved members of two self-advocacy groups in developing the standards on which the inspection was based.

There have been further instances of people with learning difficulties being involved in 'peer monitoring' or 'audit' exercises. These are usually set up as part of an internal audit within an organisation. Given appropriate preparation and support, there is great scope for involving interested people with learning difficulties as part of this kind of exercise (see box overleaf).

Working with users to improve a monitoring and review process

A monitoring and review process was established by South Glamorgan Learning Disability Joint Planning Team to undertake reviews of services provided for local people with learning difficulties. Because of local government reorganisation, the faces have changed substantially since then, but the group has been continued by the successor authority, Cardiff. Membership is multi-agency, and includes service staff, representatives of local voluntary groups, carers, and, on occasion, people with learning difficulties. The reviews are carried out using a standardised process developed for the county, and training is provided for review team members.

However, it was recognised that the process had not been directly influenced by people who use services, and tended to place undue emphasis on organisational procedures. Members of People First Cardiff and the Vale proposed developing a new set of questions which reflect things that matter to people with learning difficulties.

In response to this suggestion, a development initiative was set up. Users in eight different services were involved in a consultation process which was designed and carried out by People First members in collaboration with a facilitator. Positive and negative aspects of the service were discussed, along with ideas about what a 'perfect' service would look like. From this process the members of People First evolved a set of questions which focused on the issues that users of the service had felt to be important. These questions are now used in the reviews.

Significantly, the members of People First were paid for their contribution!

Although by no means common, there have also been examples of people with learning difficulties carrying out their *own* evaluations of services. These include:

- In 1990, the London Borough of Hillingdon commissioned two members of People First (one from Huddersfield and one from London) to carry out an evaluation of services in the borough. The pair were supported by Andrea Whittaker of the King's Fund Centre. Their results are described in a King's Fund report (Whittaker et al, 1991) which includes an 'evaluation of the evaluation'!

- London Boroughs People First obtained funding from the Joseph Rowntree Foundation to look at the way people with learning difficulties were helped to leave hospital and what their lives were like in the community. The report (Etherington et al, 1995) is available from People First.

These were both quite large-scale exercises requiring considerable resources. On a rather more modest scale, the Leeds Coalition has been working to support some former long-stay hospital residents in their efforts to take a good hard look at local services (see box below). A number of other examples of people with learning difficulties are also described in *Looking at our services* (Whittaker, 1997), produced by the King's Fund.

The Question Time Group: carrying out service checks

The Leeds Coalition is a not-for-profit organisation committed to working together to develop progressive services for adults with learning difficulties.

In 1996, the Coalition obtained funding from Leeds Health Authority to work with the Question Time Group, a group of six people with learning difficulties, then living in Meenwood Park Hospital. The Health Authority was keen to explore ways in which people with learning difficulties might be supported in carrying out service evaluations.

The group members, together with Cathy Wintersgill, a manager at the Coalition, and three independent advocates, initially spent nearly four months working on the standards by which they would judge services. Like many other evaluators, they used John O'Brien's five accomplishments (choice, presence, respect, skills and relationships) as a starting point. The aim was to work out what these ideas would mean for the group members in terms of their own lives, and then what that would mean for services. Throughout, the process was recorded using simple drawings and symbols on flip chart paper. This material was then used to group all the different issues around specific themes, with group members prioritising those that were most important to them. The results were refined and converted into a series of questions presented on A4 cards, both in writing and with an illustration.

Before the interviews, the group worked on both equal opportunities issues and confidentiality. They developed symbols for use when interviewing, to help remind each other what had been agreed. Members of the group also visited all the houses to be included in the evaluation, to check whether the people living there wanted to be interviewed.

Five residential services agreed to take part in the exercise. Working in pairs, one member would use the A4 cards to interview the people living in the house, while the other listened to the answers, which were taped. They also took photos of each house visited, to help remind the group where they had been.

After each interview there would be a de-briefing session. Subsequently, the whole group would meet and use the tapes of the interviews and de-briefing session and the photographs, to mark the house against the standards they had agreed. Finally, the group compiled a report and revisited the houses to confirm that those interviewed were happy that their words were in print.

Cathy Wintersgill is extremely positive about the experience and can point to a number of significant lessons. Using photographs was important in helping everyone (including the interviewees) to remember who was who. Similarly, the graphic recording meant that members could keep ownership of the material they generated in a far more effective way than simply using text, although one member of the group felt they were childish. Finally, Cathy points to the importance of the debriefing sessions:

> *"it was important to give group members support to talk about things when they went wrong, as well as when they went to plan."*

She hopes the exercise will have convinced local purchasers that users can and should be involved in service design, purchasing, monitoring and evaluating. She also hopes the experience will have a direct impact on the lives of the group members, possibly leaving them in a much stronger position to make informed choices about the services they use themselves.

A copy of the report can be obtained from the Leeds Coalition (see resources section).

Inspecting services

The registration and inspection of residential care services represents the main mechanism for their formal regulation. It is an area of some controversy, with learning difficulty services often subject to the same regulatory framework that was developed with large scale residential care for elderly people in mind.

Given the critical role that the arms length registration and inspection units can play, there is all the more reason to look for ways of involving people with learning difficulties in the process. There are three ways in which people who use services can have a say:

1. by being asked their views during inspections
The guidance requires inspectors to seek the views of a home's residents during an inspection. This could be made more effective; for example, residents may well be more forthcoming when an inspector is a familiar face. Similarly, prior information about inspection is important, to ensure that residents and their supporters understand what is happening.

2. by becoming 'lay' assessors
Inspection units are required to recruit and train members of the public to join them as lay members. There is no reason why these lay members cannot include

people with learning difficulties. There are a few examples of this happening now across the country. Indeed it *may* be the case that, with appropriate support, someone with learning difficulties may be able to gain the confidence of some fellow residents where professionals may not.

3. by joining advisory panels
Each registration and inspection unit is required to establish an advisory panel to assist in the regulation of services. The guidance encourages the inclusion of service users, as well as carers, members of the wider community and local home owners, although the latter are likely to be more dominant. This is an area where much more could be done to restore the balance and to ensure that the views of people with learning difficulties are recognised.

Complaints procedures

If service users are dissatisfied, an effective complaints procedure can prompt services into being more responsive to their needs. Many complaints procedures are difficult for people with learning difficulties to use (see Simons, 1995), and their involvement in developing and refining procedures could help make them more user-friendly for everyone.

Participation will involve developing more accessible materials on complaints procedures; for example, in Hackney, the head of the Registration and Inspection Unit commissioned a self-advocacy group at a local college to make the existing leaflet more accessible.

Making sure that all users know about their right to complain, and that staff understand their role in complaints procedures, will be a considerable task for most organisations, and there is much scope for involving people with learning difficulties. This can be effected through the use of videos such as *Mary Complains* and *I'm Not Complaining But ...*, both available from Pavilion Publishing (see resource section). These videos were both developed with the direct involvement of people with learning difficulties and they introduce the idea of complaining. *I'm Not Complaining But ...* could equally be used to encourage staff to look at their own practice. It also has an accompanying training pack which includes material directed at people with learning difficulties themselves who wish to become trainers.

Chapter 6: Conclusions and Policy Recommendations

"There are no quick fix solutions - grand policy statements and glossy brochures count for little. Rather, user participation is painful and 'messy' for everyone concerned. 'Bite-sized chunks', 'riddling the system', 'two steps forward, one step back', 'power imbalances', 'ongoing tensions' are all phrases that come to mind."

(Clare Evans, former Director of
Swindon and Wiltshire Users Network)

This book does not offer some nice neat solution for commissioners and purchasers to slot into place. Instead, it offers many possible options for promoting participation. Many of these will raise complex dilemmas and there are no guarantees about their effectiveness. As people find their voices, some tensions and conflict will be generated; some professionals will find themselves exposed to uncomfortable experiences in the process.

It is important to recognise that taking participation seriously will not make for an easier life. However, the alternative can only be to carry on fudging and compromising: containing situations by keeping people uniformed and uninvolved.

If all aspects of services are to be opened up to the people who use them, this will require a diversity of ways to help them get involved. It is not expected that managers and services staff will implement all the different ideas outlined in this report (that could easily become overwhelming); a balance needs to be struck between the many possibilities that exist and the need to function in the real world. Ways to optimise that balance include:

- building on the positive examples of participation that already exist locally;

- trying to embed participation in the culture of organisations so that it comes to be seen as an *integral* part of the service rather than an add-on extra;

- creating opportunities for people to share ideas and experiences so that they do not have to 'reinvent the wheel'. A consortium to pool resources could help many small authorities who would otherwise find it difficult to generate sufficient resources of their own. For example, several social services departments in the East Midlands shared the design costs of a more accessible complaints leaflet, each retaining its own logo. Some cross-organisational forums have produced work that span other authorities (see box overleaf).

65

> ## Together we can get what we want
>
> *Together we can get what we want* is a document designed to set out some of the views of people with learning difficulties who live in the West Midlands. Produced by the West Midlands Learning Disability Forum, the booklet is in a very accessible format. It is based on work by service user groups from Staffordshire, Coventry, Sandwell, Dudley, Walsall, and Wolverhampton and aims to help people with learning difficulties and staff work together to get the best service.

Structural reforms

Finally, up until this point we have largely taken as given the current legal and policy framework within which services operate. However, as the Mental Health Foundation's Committee of Enquiry into learning disability services (Mental Health Foundation, 1996) acknowledged, there is a strong case for trying not just to make the best of the current situation but also to seek substantial reforms, including:

Passage of the draft Mental Incapacity Bill into law
The adoption of the Law Commission's (1995) draft Bill on mental incapacity would clarify the currently confused situation in relation to competence. It would both confirm people's rights to self-determination *and* provide an additional measure of protection. In this light, *Who Decides?*, the recent Green Paper (Lord Chancellor's Department, 1997), is a welcome contribution to the debate.

Implementation of Sections 1 and 2 of the 1986 Disabled Person's Act
Sections 1 and 2 of the 1986 Disabled Person's Act gave individuals the right to appoint an advocate, and required the development of advocacy schemes by all local authorities. However, these sections of the act were never implemented; the then Conservative government argued that their provisions had been overtaken by the 1990 NHS and Community Care Act. However, the latter does not require services to recognise advocates appointed by people who use services. There have been many calls for the full implementation of the 1986 act, the latest being the Committee of Inquiry established by the Mental Health Foundation (1996). In the meantime, there is an argument for ensuring that all contracts for services specify the right of individuals to have an advocate, and for advocates to have unrestricted access to their partners.

Establishment of appropriate guidance for complaints procedures in independent sector services
There is now quite extensive official guidance on complaints procedures in social services departments. Similarly, although it is too early to tell how well they are working, the reformed complaints procedures in the NHS have also been the subject of extensive documentation. However, there is much less guidance on how

complaints procedures in the independent sector services should work (see Chapter 5). There is an urgent need for further work in this area, along with a clear statement from Government about minimum requirements. In the meantime, commissioners and purchasers could specify minimum standards for complaints handling, through the contracting process.

Reform of both the benefit rules and regulatory mechanisms to make it easier for people with learning difficulties to live in their own home and to take paid employment

The current benefits system, including not just social security but housing subsidies, does not promote choice. Instead, it often limits choice, forcing people to use particular kinds of services whether they suit them or not. It *is* possible to enable some individuals to live in their own homes, and to help some people find paid work. However, due to the way the system currently works (see Simons, 1998) these are options that only a minority of people have been able to access. Perhaps even worse, the bizarre logic of the benefits system has meant that some people have had to choose between having their own home and having a paid job.

Services which really begin to involve people with learning difficulties in decision making will soon find that many will be asking for just these options and that the wider policy framework will limit the extent to which they can deliver them. Ensuring that the concerns of people with learning difficulties and their supporters are known and understood by policy makers is a key role for the wider service community, as is ensuring that people with learning difficulties themselves get a chance to be heard.

A fundamental notion underpinning this book has been the principle that people with learning difficulties are, first and foremost, *citizens*. The key roles of specialist learning disability services, therefore, involve both enabling people with learning difficulties to exercise their *rights* as citizens and to discharge the responsibilities that, as citizens, we all have. Participation in its widest sense is very much bound up with citizenship; to be an active citizen is to be involved not only in decisions about one's own life, but also to play an active role in one's community. Retaining this vision of participation as citizenship (not simply 'user-ship') is key to the whole enterprise.

Bibliography

Bewley, C. and Glendinning, C. (1994) *Involving disabled people in community care planning.* York: Joseph Rowntree Foundation/Community Care.

Beyer, S. (1996) The All Wales Strategy: what people said. *Llais,* 42, Autumn, 3-5.

Brandon, D. (1994) *Money for change.* Cambridge: Anglia Polytechnic University.

Brown, H. (1996) Editorial. *Tizard Learning Disability Review*, 1,2, 7-8.

Cambridge, P. (1996) *The sexuality and sexual rights of people with learning disability: considerations for staff and carers.* Kidderminster: BILD Publications.

Challis, D. and Davies, B. (1993) Case management studies: an overview of the Kent, Gateshead and Lewisham findings, in D. Robbins (ed.) *Community care: findings from the Department of Health funded research 1988-92.* London: HMSO.

Craft, A. (1996) Abuse of younger and older people: similarities and differences, in R. Clough (ed.) *The abuse of care in residential institutions.* London: Whiting and Birch/SCA Education.

Dook, J., Honess, J. and Senker, J. (1997) *Service brokerage in Southwark.* London: Choice Publications.

Dowson, S. (1995) *Means to control: a review of service brokerage models in community care.* London: Values Into Action.

Dowson, S. (1997) Empowerment within services; a comfortable delusion, in P. Ramcharan, G. Roberts, G. Grant and J. Borland (eds) *Empowerment in everyday life.* London: Jessica Kingsley.

Dowson, S. and Whittaker, A. (1993) *On one side: the role of the adviser in supporting people with learning difficulties in self-advocacy groups.* London: Values Into Action in association with the King's Fund Centre.

Duffy, S. (1996) *Unlocking the imagination: purchasing services for people with learning difficulties.* London: Choice Publications.

Ellis, K. (1993) *Squaring the circle: user and carer participation in needs assessment.* York: Joseph Rowntree Foundation.

Emerson, E. and Hatton, C. (1998) Residential provision for people with intellectual disabilities in England, Wales and Scotland. *Journal of Applied Research in Intellectual Disabilities,* 11,1, 1-14.

Etherington, A., Stocker, B. and Whittaker, A. (1995) *Outside but not inside - yet.* London: People First.

Evans, C. (1997) Doing it for ourselves. *Community Care,* 29 May, Inside supplement, 1.

Felce, D. (1996) The quality of support for ordinary living: resident interactions and resident activity, in J. Mansell and K. Ericsson (eds) *Deinstitutionalization and community living: intellectual disability services in Britain, Scandinavia and the USA.* London: Chapman and Hall.

Grant, G. (1997) Consulting to involve, or consulting to empower, in P. Ramcharan, G. Roberts, G. Grant and J. Borland (eds) *Empowerment in everyday life.* London: Jessica Kingsley.

Greig, R. (1997) Joint commissioning: searching for stability in an unstable world. *Tizard Learning Disability Review,* 2,1, 19-26.

Greig, R., Cambridge, P. and Rucker, L. (1996) Care management and joint commissioning, in J. Harris (ed.) *Purchasing services for people with learning disabilities, challenging behaviour and mental health needs.* Kidderminster: British Institute of Learning Disabilities, Seminar Papers No. 6.

Hackney Social Services (1995) *A new sense of direction.* London: Hackney Social Services.

Harris, J. (1996) *Purchasing services for people with learning disabilities, challenging behaviour and mental health needs.* Kidderminster: British Institute of Learning Disabilities, Seminar Papers No. 6.

Holman, A. and Collins, J. (1997) *Funding freedom: direct payments for people with learning difficulties.* London: Values Into Action.

Hoyes, L. and Means, R. (1994) Obstacle races. *Community Care,* 19 May, 22-23.

Keeble, M. (1996) *"It seems like common sense to me": supported housing tenants having a say.* Cardiff: Tenant Participation Advisory Service (Wales) and Joseph Rowntree Foundation.

King's Fund (1980) *An ordinary life.* London: King's Fund Centre.

King, N. (1996) *Ownership options: a guide to home ownership for people with learning disabilities.* London: National Federation of Housing Associations.

Kinsella, P. (1993) *Supported living - a new paradigm?* Manchester: National Development Team.

LA(96)10, *Children services planning: Local authority circular 10*, 27th March, 1996. London: Department of Health.

Law Commission (1995) *Mental incapacity.* London: HMSO.

Lindow, V. and Morris, J. (1995) *User involvement: synthesis of findings and experience in the field of community care.* York: Joseph Rowntree Foundation

Lord Chancellor's Department (1997) *Who decides? Making decisions on behalf of mentally incapacitated adults.* London: The Stationery Office.

McCarthy, M. and Cambridge, P. (1996) *Your rights about sex.* Kidderminster: BILD Publications.

McGowan, C. (1996) Seeing is commissioning. *Community Care,* 25 April.

Mental Health Foundation (1996) *Building expectations: opportunities and services for people with a learning disability.* London: Mental Health Foundation.

Mount, B. (1994) Benefits and limitations of personal futures planning, in V. J. Bradley, J. W. Asbough and B. C. Blaney (eds) *Creating individual supports for people with developmental disabilities: a mandate for change at many levels.* Baltimore: Paul Brookes.

NWTDT (1996) *Partners in Policymaking.* Calderstones: North West Training and Development Team.

O'Brien, J. and Lovett, H. (1992) *Finding a way towards everyday lives: the contribution of person-centred planning.* Harrisburg, Pennsylvania: Pennsylvania Office of Mental Retardation.

People First (1993) *Oi! It's my assessment. Why not listen to me!* London: People First.

Richardson, A. (1993) *Participation.* London: Routledge and Kegan Paul.

Roberts, G. (1997) Capacity and Empowerment, in P. Ramcharan, G. Roberts, G. Grant and J. Borland (eds) *Empowerment in everyday life.* London: Jessica Kingsley.

Robinson, C. and Simons, K. (1996) *In safe hands? Quality and regulation in adult placement services for adults with learning difficulties.* Sheffield: University of Sheffield Joint Unit for Social Services Research Monographs.

Robinson, C. and Williams, V. (1997) *A view from the top: the views of senior managers on the implementation of the Carers Act 1995. Report on first stage of the research.* Bristol: Norah Fry Research Centre.

Sanderson, H., Kennedy, J., Ritchie, P. and Goodwin, G. (1997) *People, plans and possibilities: exploring person-centred planning.* Edinburgh: Scottish Human Services Ltd.

Simons, K. (1993) *Citizen advocacy: the inside view.* Bristol: Norah Fry Research Centre.

Simons, K. (1995) *I'm not complaining, but ... Complaints procedures in social services departments.* York: Joseph Rowntree Foundation.

Simons, K. (1997) *Whose home is this? Tenant participation in supported housing.* Brighton: Pavilion Publishing.

Simons, K. (1998) *Home, work and inclusion. The social policy implications of supported living and employment for people with learning disabilities.* York: York Publishing Services.

Simons, K. and Ward, L. (1997) *A foot in the door: the early years of supported living in the UK.* Brighton: Pavilion Publishing/National Development Team.

Smull, M. and Harrison, S. (1992) *Supporting people with severe reputations in the community.* Virginia: National Association of State Mental Retardation Programme Directors.

SSI (1991a) *Care management and assessment: manager's guide.* London: HMSO.

SSI (1991b) *The right to complain: practice guidance on complaints procedures.* London: HMSO.

SSI (1995) *Opportunity or knocks: national inspection of recreation and leisure in day services for people with learning difficulties.* London: Department of Health.

Sutcliffe, J. and Simons, K. (1993) *Self advocacy and adults with learning difficulties.* Leicester: National Institute of Adult Continuing Education.

Townsley, R. and Macadam, M. (1996) *Choosing staff.* Bristol: Policy Press.

Townsley, R., Howarth, J., Le Grys, P. and Macadam, M. (1997) *Getting involved in choosing staff.* Brighton: Pavilion Publishing.

Turner, S., Sweeney, D. and Hayes, L. (1995) *Developments in community care for adults with learning disabilities: a review of 1993/4 community care plans.* Manchester: Hester Adrian Research Centre.

Warburton, W. (1990) *Developing services for disabled people.* London: Social Services Inspectorate, Department of Health.

Ward, L. (1997) *Seen and heard: involving disabled children and young people in research and development projects.* York: Joseph Rowntree Foundation.

Wertheimer, A. (1995) *Circles of support: building inclusive communities.* Bristol: Circles Network UK.

Wertheimer, A. (1996) *Changing days: developing new day opportunities for people who have learning difficulties.* London: King's Fund.

West Midlands Learning Disability Forum (1995) *Together we can get what we want.* Kidderminster: BILD Publications.

Whittaker, A., Gardner, S. and Kershaw, J. (1991) *Service evaluation by people with learning difficulties.* London: King's Fund Centre.

Whittaker, A. (1997) *Looking at our services: service evaluations by people with learning difficulties.* London: King's Fund.

Other Material of Interest

Beresford, P. and Harding, T. (1993) *A challenge to change: practical experience of building user-led services.* London: National Institute for Social Work.

Brandon, D., with Brandon, A. and Brandon, T. (1995) *Advocacy: power to people with disabilities.* Birmingham: Venture Press.

Fielder, B. (1993) *Getting results: unlocking community care in partnership with disabled people.* London: King's Fund Centre and the Prince of Wales' Advisory Group on Disability, Living Options Partnership Paper No. 1.

Harding, T. and Beresford, P. (1996) *The standards we expect - what service users and carers want from social service workers.* London: National Institute for Social Work.

Herd, D. and Stalker, K. (1996) *Involving disabled people in services.* Edinburgh: Social Work Inspectorate.

Jack, R. (1995) *Empowerment in community care.* London: Chapman and Hall.

Lewis, J. (1996) *Towards equality for black and ethnic minority people with learning difficulties.* London: Choice Press.

Lindow, V. (1996) *Community care service users as consultants and trainers.* London: Department of Health.

Moffatt, V. (1996) *How to help people with learning difficulties understand what you're saying.* London: Choice Press.

Morris, J. (1994) *The shape of things to come? User-led social services.* London: National Institute for Social Work.

Morris, J. (1995) *The power to change: commissioning health and social services with disabled people.* London: King's Fund Centre and the Prince of Wales' Advisory Group on Disability, Living Options Partnership Paper No. 1.

Morris, J. (1996) *Encouraging user involvement in commissioning: a resource for commissioners.* London: Department of Health.

Mosley, J. (1994) '*You choose: a handbook for staff working with people who have learning disabilities to promote self-esteem and self-advocacy.* Wisbech: LDA.

Winn, L. (1990) *Power to the people: the key to responsive services in health and social care.* London: King's Fund Centre.

Resource Section

Advocacy in Action
30 Addison Street
Arboretum
Nottingham   NG1 4HA

Tel: 0115 947 0780

Bristol and District People First
Easton Business Park
Felix Road
Easton
Bristol   BS5 0HE

Tel: 0117 941 5842

British Council of Disabled People
Litchurch Plaza
Litchurch Lane
Derby   DE24 8AA

Tel: 01332 298288
Fax: 01332 295580

British Institute of Learning Disabilities (BILD)
Wolverhampton Rd
Kidderminster
Worcester   DY10 3PP

Tel: 01562 850251
Fax: 01562 851970
E-mail: bild@bild.demon.co.uk
http//www.bild.org.uk

Change
First Floor
69/85 Old Street
London   EC1V 9HY

Tel: 0171 490 2668
Fax: 0171 490 3581
E-mail: contact@changeuk.demon.co.uk

Circles Network
Pamwell House
160 Pennywell Road
Upper Easton
Bristol   BS5 0TX

Tel: 0117 939 3917
Fax: 0117 939 3918

Citizen Advocacy Information and Training
Unit 164 Lee Valley Technopark
Ashley Road
Tottenham Hale
London   N17 9LN

Tel: 0181 880 4545
Fax: 0181 880 4113

Community Care Development Centre
King's College
Friars House
157-168 Blackfriars Road
London   SE1 8EZ

Tel: 0171 928 7994
Fax: 0171 928 4101

Connect
Phoenix NHS Trust
Brentry
Charlton Road
Westbury-on-Trim
Bristol   BS10 6JH

Tel: 0117 908 8475
Fax: 0117 950 5606
E-mail:
connect-infor@compuserve.com

East Midlands Further Education Council (EMFEC)
Robins Wood House
Robins Wood Road
Aspley
Nottingham   NG8 3NH

Tel: 0115 929 3291
Fax: 0115 929 9393
E-mail: enquiries@emfec.co.uk

Europe People First
c/o Bristol and District People First
Easton Business Park
Felix Road
Easton
Bristol   BS5 0HE

Tel: 0117 941 5842

Information Exchange on Self Advocacy and Participation
c/o Andrea Whittaker
King's Fund
Development Centre
11-13 Cavendish Square
London   WlM 0AN

Tel: 0171 307 2400
Fax: 0171 307 2810

Joseph Rowntree Foundation
The Homestead
40 Water End
York   Y03 6LP

Tel: 01904 629241
Fax: 01904 620072
http//www.jrf.org.uk

King's Fund Centre
11-13 Cavendish Square
London   W1M OAN

Tel: 0171 307 2400
Fax: 0171 307 2810

Leeds Coalition
Bridge House
Balm Rd
Hunslet
Leeds   LS10 2TP

Tel: 0113 270 3233
Tel: 0113 270 3733

London Boroughs People First
Instrument House
207-215 King's Cross Rd
London   WCIX 9DB

Tel: 0171 713 6400

MacIntyre Care
602 South Seventh Street
Central Milton Keynes   MK9 2JA

Tel: 01908 230100
Fax: 01908 695643

National Centre for Independent Living
250 Kennington Lane
London   SE11 5RD

Tel: 0171 587 1663
Fax: 0171 582 2469

National Development Team
St. Peter's Court
8 Trumpet Street
Manchester   M1 5LW

Tel: 0161 228 7055
Fax: 0161 228 7059
E-mail: office@ndt.org.uk

National Institute for Social Work
5 Tavistock Place
London   WC1H 9SN

Tel: 0171 387 9681
Fax: 0171 387 7968
http//www.nisw.org.uk/

National Institute of Adult Continuing Education (NIACE)
21 De Montfort Street
Leicester   LE1 7GE

Tel: 0116 204 4200/1
Fax: 0116 285 4514
E-mail: enquiries@niace.org.uk
http//www.niace.org.uk

Norah Fry Research Centre
University of Bristol
3 Priory Road
Bristol   BS8 1TX

Tel: 0117 923 8137
Fax: 0117 946 6553
http://www.bris.ac.uk/Depts/NorahFry/

Northampton People First
PO Box 5200
Northampton
NN1 1ZB

Tel: 01604 637233
Fax: 01604 603503
E-mail: northhants@peoplefirst.org.uk
http://www.peoplefirst.org.uk/

North West Training and Development Team
Calderstones
Whalley
Clitheroe   BB7 9PE

Tel: 01254 821334
Fax: 01254 821329

The Quality Network
Oxfordshire Learning Disabilities NHS Trust
Slade House
Horspath Driftway
Headington
Oxford   OX3 7JH

Tel: 01865 228186
Fax: 01865 228182

Pavilion Publishing
8 St George's Place
Brighton
East Sussex   BN1 4GB

Tel: 01273 623222
Fax: 01273 625526
E.mail: Pavpub@pavilion.co.uk

People First Cardiff and the Vale
c/o DART
Friary Centre
The Friary
Cardiff   CF1 4AA

Tel: 01222 644696

Pete Le Grys - Development Officer
Consumer Relations Department
Phoenix NHS Trust
Brentry
Charlton Road
Westbury-on-Trym
Bristol   BS10 6JH

Tel: 0117 908 8478

POhWER
Unit 13 Chells Enterprise Village
Chells Way
Chells
Stevenage   SG2 0LZ

Tel: 01438 740162
Fax/Text: 01438 351297
E-mail: pohwer@globalnet.co.uk

Scottish Human Services (SHS) Ltd
1A Washington Court
Washington Lane
Edinburgh   EH11 2HA

Tel: 0131 538 7717
Fax: 0131 538 7719

SCOVO
5 Dock Chambers
Bute Street
Cardiff   CF1 6AG

Tel: 01222 492443
Fax: 01222 481043

Skills for People (START video)
Key House
Tankerville Place
Newcastle upon Tyne
NE2 3AT

Tel: 0191 281 8737
Fax: 0191 212 0300

**Southwark Consortium
(now Choice Support)**
27 Barry Rd
London   SE22 0HX

Tel: 0181 693 6088
Fax: 0181 299 4818

Swindon People First
The Health Hydro
Milton Road
Swindon   SN1 5JA

Tel: 01793 465630

Values Into Action
Oxford House
Derbyshire St.
London   E2 6HG

Tel: 0171 729 5436
Fax: 0171 729 7797
E-mail: VIA@BTInternet.com
http://www.demon.co.uk/via/

**Welsh Centre for Learning
Disability Applied Research Unit**
Meridian Court
North Road
Cardiff   CF4 3BL

Tel: 01222 691795
Fax: 01222 610812

West Surrey Health Authority
The Ridgewood Centre
Old Bisley Road
Frimley
Camberley
Surrey   GU16 5QE

Tel: 01276 671718
Fax: 01276 605491
E-mail:
west.surrey.health@dial.pipex.com